1st EDITION

Perspectives on Diseases and Disorders

Sudden Infant Death Syndrome

Jacqueline Langwith
Book Editor

Detroit • New York • San Francisco • New Haven, Conn • Waterville, Maine • London

Elizabeth Des Chenes, *Managing Editor*

LIBRARY OF CONGRESS CATALOGING-IN-PUBLICATION DATA

Sudden infant death syndrome / Jacqueline Langwith, book editor.
   p. ; cm. -- (Perspectives on diseases and disorders)
  Includes bibliographical references and index.
  ISBN 978-0-7377-5784-2 (hardcover)
  1. Sudden infant death syndrome--Etiology. 2. Sudden infant death syndrome--Physiological aspects. I. Langwith, Jacqueline. II. Series: Perspectives on diseases and disorders.
  [DNLM: 1. Sudden Infant Death--etiology. 2. Sudden Infant Death--prevention & control. 3. Pacifiers--contraindications. 4. Serotonin--physiology. 5. Sleep--physiology. WS 430]
  RJ320.S93S818 2011
  618.92'026--dc22
                                 2011011656

Printed in the United States of America
1 2 3 4 5 6 7 15 14 13 12 11

CONTENTS

FOREWORD

"Medicine, to produce health, has to examine disease."
—Plutarch

Independent research on a health issue is often the first step to complement discussions with a physician. But locating accurate, well-organized, understandable medical information can be a challenge. A simple Internet search on terms such as "cancer" or "diabetes," for example, returns an intimidating number of results. Sifting through the results can be daunting, particularly when some of the information is inconsistent or even contradictory. The Greenhaven Press series Perspectives on Diseases and Disorders offers a solution to the often overwhelming nature of researching diseases and disorders.

From the clinical to the personal, titles in the Perspectives on Diseases and Disorders series provide students and other researchers with authoritative, accessible information in unique anthologies that include basic information about the disease or disorder, controversial aspects of diagnosis and treatment, and first-person accounts of those impacted by the disease. The result is a well-rounded combination of primary and secondary sources that, together, provide the reader with a better understanding of the disease or disorder.

Each volume in Perspectives on Diseases and Disorders explores a particular disease or disorder in detail. Material for each volume is carefully selected from a wide range of sources, including encyclopedias, journals, newspapers, nonfiction books, speeches, government documents, pamphlets, organization newsletters, and position papers. Articles in the first chapter provide an authoritative, up-to-date overview that covers symptoms, causes and effects, treatments, cures, and medical advances. The second chapter presents a substantial number of opposing viewpoints on controversial treatments and other current debates relating to the volume topic. The third chapter offers a variety of personal perspectives on the disease or disorder. Patients, doctors, caregivers, and loved ones represent just some of the voices found in this narrative chapter.

Each Perspectives on Diseases and Disorders volume also includes:

- An **annotated table of contents** that provides a brief summary of each article in the volume.

- An **introduction** specific to the volume topic.

- Full-color **charts and graphs** to illustrate key points, concepts, and theories.

- Full-color **photos** that show aspects of the disease or disorder and enhance textual material.

- **"Fast Facts"** that highlight pertinent additional statistics and surprising points.

- A **glossary** providing users with definitions of important terms.

- A **chronology** of important dates relating to the disease or disorder.

- An annotated list of **organizations to contact** for students and other readers seeking additional information.

- A **bibliography** of additional books and periodicals for further research.

- A detailed **subject index** that allows readers to quickly find the information they need.

Whether a student researching a disorder, a patient recently diagnosed with a disease, or an individual who simply wants to learn more about a particular disease or disorder, a reader who turns to Perspectives on Diseases and Disorders will find a wealth of information in each volume that offers not only basic information, but also vigorous debate from multiple perspectives.

INTRODUCTION

New parents, particularly mothers, confront an array of difficult parenting questions soon after their babies are born. Should I breast-feed my baby? Should I vaccinate my baby? Should I give my baby a pacifier? The risk of sudden infant death syndrome (SIDS) often looms large in the minds of parents as they answer these and many other questions. Whether or not to give a baby a pacifier has been the subject of a debate in the medical community. In the past, most health-care professionals discouraged the use of pacifiers because they can have adverse health effects and interfere with breast-feeding; however, many physicians are rethinking this advice because there is evidence suggesting that pacifier use can reduce the risk of SIDS.

The modern pacifier was invented in 1900, although parents have always tried to soothe their babies by placing something in their mouths. In earlier times parents tied cloth around balls of sugar, bread, or fat and used these to soothe their babies. Modern pacifiers are based on C.W. Meinecke's design for a "baby comforter," which was patented in the United States in 1900. Today, pacifiers are an accepted, and to some parents, an essential, component of baby care. It is hardly surprising to see babies with their "binky" in their mouth, and typically diaper bags contain several, in case one is dropped.

Despite their widespread use, pacifiers have been associated with adverse health effects. In the United States and England in the early 1900s, they were associated with the poorer classes and called menaces to health by some. More recently, doctors discouraged their use because they could interfere with breast-feeding. Babies who are given

Whether to use a pacifier to calm a fussy baby has been a subject of debate within the medical community since the item was first introduced in 1900.
(© Judith Collins/Alamy)

pacifiers at an early age may have difficulty breast-feeding, causing frustration for mother and child. Some babies may even refuse to breast-feed because of pacifier use. Pacifiers have also been associated with later dental problems and ear infections.

The idea that pacifiers could prevent SIDS was postulated several decades ago. In 1979 three Italian researchers suggested that pacifiers, called "dummies" or "soothers" in other countries, might be able to prevent SIDS. During the 1990s and the 2000s, several studies provided evidence supporting the Italian researchers' suggestion. For instance, a study published in the December 2005 issue of the *British Medical Journal* found that babies who used a pacifier had a 92 percent decreased chance of SIDS. For the study, De-kun Li and his colleagues interviewed nearly 500 parents in Northern California, including 185 whose children had died from SIDS. All the parents were asked about their babies' pacifier use during sleep and for those whose children had died from SIDS, particularly whether their baby had a pacifier during their "last sleep." Only 4 percent of the babies who died of SIDS had been using a pacifier, while 24 percent of babies who had slept safely had been using a pacifier. When asked about the study, Ian Holzman, chief of newborn medicine at Mount Sinai Medical Center in New York, responded that "almost every study is showing the same thing, which makes one think it may well be true. Pacifiers have got to be the cheapest medical intervention for something in a long time."[1]

Although the evidence links pacifiers to a reduced SIDS risk, exactly how they exert their protective effect is still unclear. The Italian researchers believed pacifiers might prevent SIDS by keeping a baby's airway open. In October 2010 a study at Monash University in Australia presented evidence that pacifiers prevent SIDS by changing sleep patterns and keeping babies in a light sleep where they are more easily aroused. As of January 2011, there is no universally accepted explanation for why pacifiers seem to prevent SIDS.

In 2005 the American Academy of Pediatrics (AAP) determined that the evidence was strong enough to begin recommending that parents consider offering their baby a pacifier at nap time and bedtime as a way to reduce the risk of SIDS. According to the AAP SIDS Task Force headed by researcher Fern R. Hauck, "Although the mechanism is not known, the reduced risk of SIDS associated with pacifier use during sleep is compelling, and the evidence that pacifier use inhibits breastfeeding or causes later dental complications is not. Until evidence dictates otherwise, the task force recommends use of a pacifier throughout the first year of life."[2] The AAP provided specific procedures that parents should use when offering pacifiers, such as that they should not be reinserted if they fall out, they should not be coated with sweeteners, and pacifier introduction should be delayed until one month of age for breast-fed infants to ensure that breast-feeding is firmly established.

At the time many pediatricians and researchers believed the AAP's recommendations were ill advised. These physicians generally reasoned that the evidence supporting pacifiers' protective effect in regard to SIDS was not strong enough to outweigh the negative effects that pacifiers may cause. The opponents of the recommendation disagreed that the studies that the AAP used to support its recommendation actually proved that pacifiers protect from SIDS. The studies showed that nonuse of a pacifier was associated with SIDS, opponents argued, but not that the pacifier prevented SIDS. Boston-based physicians Alison Stuebe and Kimberly Lee claimed that it was "far from clear" that "pacifiers play a causal role in SIDS." The physicians assert that there were many scenarios where a baby who died from SIDS may not have had a pacifier, but it did not mean the absence of a pacifier contributed to the SIDS death. They stated as an example, "Consider an infant with a viral illness and a decreased arousal threshold who then falls asleep in a caregiver's arms without his or her pacifier. Later that night, with arousal dampened by the illness, the infant dies as a result of SIDS. In this case, 'no pacifier in last sleep' is a marker for decreased arousal." The two doctors went on to say that "the consistent association between pacifier use at last sleep and reduced SIDS risk is interesting. However, we disagree with the assertion that there is adequate evidence to recommend universal pacifier use."[3] Italian physicians Roberto Buzzetti and Roberto D'Amico also believed the studies were inadequate to support the AAP's recommendation. "In the absence of clear and strong evidence in support of the use of pacifiers (which could have some adverse effects on breastfeeding), we think it would be more appropriate not to provide any recommendations,"[4] responded the doctors.

Several years later physicians are still debating the wisdom of the AAP's pacifier recommendations. In the May

2009 issue of *American Family Physician,* Stephen Adams, Matthew Good, and Gina DeFranco reviewed the risks of SIDS and reiterated the AAP's pacifier recommendations. This prompted husband-and-wife doctors David and Katherine Abdun-Nur to respond. In a letter to the editor published in the September 2010 issue of *American Family Physician,* they wrote, "The original studies that linked pacifier use to a decrease in SIDS were all based on observational data, meaning they prove only an association, not cause and effect. Pacifiers have their place in soothing irritated babies, but their use should not be encouraged, as they cause real problems with breastfeeding."

The debate about whether or not pacifiers reduce the risk of SIDS is a contentious issue. In *Perspectives on Diseases and Disorders: Sudden Infant Death Syndrome,* other debates about SIDS are presented, along with an overview of what scientists know and do not know about SIDS, and the personal stories of those who have lost children to this mysterious disease.

Notes

1 Quoted in Amanda Gardner, "Pacifiers Prevent SIDS Deaths: Study," *HealthDay News,* December 8, 2005.
2 Fern R. Hauck et al., "Do Pacifiers Reduce the Risk of Sudden Infant Death Syndrome? A Meta-Analysis," *Pediatrics,* November 2005.
3 Alison Stuebe and Kimberly Lee, "The Pacifier Debate," Letters to the Editor, *Pediatrics,* May 2006.
4 Roberto Buzzetti and Roberto D'Amico, "The Pacifier Debate," Letters to the Editor, *Pediatrics,* May 2006.

CHAPTER 1

Understanding Sudden Infant Death Syndrome

An Overview of Sudden Infant Death Syndrome

Teresa Odle and Jacqueline L. Longe

In the following viewpoint, Teresa Odle and Jacqueline L. Longe provide an overview of sudden infant death syndrome (SIDS), a tragic and medically baffling medical disorder that causes the sudden death of otherwise healthy infants. Although the exact cause of SIDS is unknown, Odle and Longe say that scientists have identified several risk factors and several things parents can do to try to prevent SIDS from occurring. Teresa Odle and Jacqueline L. Longe are nationally published medical writers.

S udden infant death syndrome (SIDS) is the unexplained death without warning of an apparently healthy infant, usually during sleep.

Also known as crib death, SIDS has baffled physicians and parents for years. In the 1990s, advances have been made in preventing the occurrence of SIDS, which killed more than 4,800 babies in 1992 and 3,279 infants in 1995.

SOURCE: Teresa Odle and Jacqueline L. Longe, "Sudden Infant Death Syndrome," *Gale Encyclopedia of Medicine,* 3d ed. Copyright © 2006 Gale, a part of Cengage Learning, Inc. Reproduced by permission.

Photo on facing page. A giant red nose adorns the famous Mr. Moon Face in Melbourne, Australia, during a fund-raising event sponsored by SIDS and Kids Victoria, a nonprofit SIDS-awareness and family support organization. **(William West/AFP/Getty Images)**

Education programs aimed at encouraging parents and caregivers to place babies on their backs and sides when putting them to bed have helped contribute to a lower mortality rate from SIDS.

In the United States, SIDS strikes 0.57 in every thousand, making it the third leading cause of death in newborns. It accounts for about 8% of deaths occurring during the first year of life. SIDS most commonly affects babies between the ages of two months and six months; it almost never strikes infants younger than two weeks of age or older than eight months. Most SIDS deaths occur between midnight and 8 AM. Although placing babies on their backs has greatly decreased the incidence of SIDS, and despite a robust public health campaign to educate parents about the importance of "Back to Sleep," about 13% of babies are still placed on their stomachs to sleep.

Key SIDS Characteristics

SIDS is a defined medical disorder that is listed in the International Classification of Diseases, 9th Revision (ICD-9). The first published research about sudden infant death appeared in the mid-nineteenth century. Since then, researchers and healthcare providers have struggled to define the syndrome and determine its causes. The key characteristics of SIDS include:

- infant less than one year of age
- infant seemingly healthy (no preceding symptoms)
- complete investigation fails to find a cause of death
- no associated child abuse or illness

The exact causes of SIDS are still unknown, although studies have shown that many of the infants had recently been under a doctor's care for a cold or other illness of the upper respiratory tract. Most SIDS deaths occur during the winter and early spring, which are the peak times for respiratory infections. The most common risk factors for SIDS include:

- sleeping on the stomach (in the prone position)
- mother who smokes during pregnancy; smokers are as much as three times more likely than nonsmokers to have a SIDS baby
- the presence of passive smoke in the household
- male sex; the male/female ratio in SIDS deaths is 3:2;
- belonging to an economically deprived or minority family
- mother under 20 years of age at pregnancy
- mother who abuses drugs
- mother with little or no prenatal care
- prematurity or low weight at birth
- family history of SIDS

Most of these risk factors are associated with significantly higher rates of SIDS; however, none of them are exact enough to be useful in predicting which specific children may die from SIDS.

Theories About SIDS

Currently, it is not known whether the immediate cause of death from SIDS is a heart problem or a sudden interruption of breathing. The most consistent autopsy findings are pinpoint hemorrhages inside the baby's chest and mild inflammation or congestion of the nose, throat, and airway. Some doctors have thought that the children stop breathing because their upper airway gets blocked. Others have suggested that the children have an abnormally high blood level of the chemicals that transmit nerve impulses to the brain, or that there is too much fetal hemoglobin in the blood. A third theory concerns the possibility that SIDS infants have an underlying abnormality in the central nervous system. This suggestion is based on the assumption that normal infants sense when their air supply is inadequate and wake up. Babies with an abnormal nervous system, however, do not have the same

FAST FACT

According to the US Centers for Disease Control and Prevention, each year about forty-six hundred US infants die suddenly of no immediately obvious cause.

Research has shown that mothers who smoke are as much as three times more likely than nonsmokers to have a SIDS baby. (AJPhoto/Photo Researchers, Inc.)

alarm mechanism in their brains. Other theories about the cause of death in SIDS include immune system disorders that cause changes in the baby's heart rate and breathing patterns during sleep, or a metabolic disorder that causes a buildup of fatty acids in the baby's system.

A recent theory proposes that SIDS is connected to the child's rebreathing of stale air trapped in soft bedding. In addition to the infant's sleeping in the prone position, pillows, sheepskins, and other soft items may contribute to trapping air around the baby's mouth and nose, which causes the baby to breathe in too much carbon dioxide and not enough oxygen. Wrapping a baby too warmly has also been proposed as a factor.

Diagnosis, Treatment, and Prevention

The diagnosis of SIDS is primarily a diagnosis of exclusion. This means that it is given only after other possible causes of the baby's death have been ruled out. Known risk factors aid in the diagnosis. Unlike the pattern in other diseases, however, the diagnosis of SIDS can only be given postmortem. It is recommended that all infants who die in their sleep receive an autopsy to determine the cause. Autopsies indicate a definite explanation in about 20% of cases of sudden infant death. In addition, an autopsy can often put to rest any doubts the parents may have. Investigation of the location of the death is also useful in determining the child's sleeping position, bedding, room temperature, and similar factors.

There is no treatment for SIDS, only identification of risk factors and preventive measures. The baby's parents may benefit from referral to counseling and support groups for parents of SIDS victims.

SIDS appears to be at least partly preventable, which has been shown by a substantial decrease in the case rate. The following are recommended as preventive measures:

Sleep position. The United States Department of Health and Human Services initiated a "Back-to-Sleep" campaign in 1994 to educate the public about sleep position. Prior to that time, an estimated 70% of infants slept on their stomachs, since parents had been taught that a "back down" position contributed to choking during sleep. There are some conditions for which doctors will recommend the prone position, but for normal infants, side or back (supine) positions are better. When placing an infant on his or her side, the parent should pull the child's lower arm forward so that he or she is less likely to roll over onto the stomach. When babies are awake and being observed, they should be placed on their stomachs frequently to aid in the development of the muscles and skills involved in lifting the head. Once a baby can roll over to his or her stomach, he or she has developed to the point where the risk of SIDS is minimal.

Good prenatal care. Proper prenatal care can help prevent the abnormalities that put children at higher risk for SIDS. Mothers who do not receive prenatal care are also more likely to have premature and low birth-weight babies. Expectant mothers should also be warned about the risks of smoking, alcohol intake, and drug use during pregnancy.

Proper bedding. Studies have shown that soft bedding, such as beanbags, waterbeds and soft mattresses, contributes to SIDS. Babies should sleep on firm mattresses with no soft or fluffy materials underneath or around them— including quilts, pillows, thick comforters or lambskin. Soft stuffed toys should not be placed in the crib while babies sleep.

Room temperature. Although babies should be kept warm, they do not need to be any warmer than is comfortable for the caregiver. An overheated baby is more likely to sleep deeply, perhaps making it more difficult to wake when short of breath. Room temperature and wrapping should keep the baby warm and comfortable but not overheated.

Diet. Some studies indicate that breastfed babies are at lower risk for SIDS. It is thought that the mother's milk may provide additional immunity to the infections that can trigger sudden death in infants.

Bedsharing with parents. Opinions differ on whether or not bedsharing of infant and mother increases or decreases the risk of SIDS. Bedsharing may encourage breastfeeding or alter sleep patterns, which could lower the risk of SIDS. On the other hand, some studies suggest that bedsharing

Infant Mortality and Sudden Infant Death Syndrome Rates, 1983–2005

Based on data from US Centers for Disease Control and Prevention.

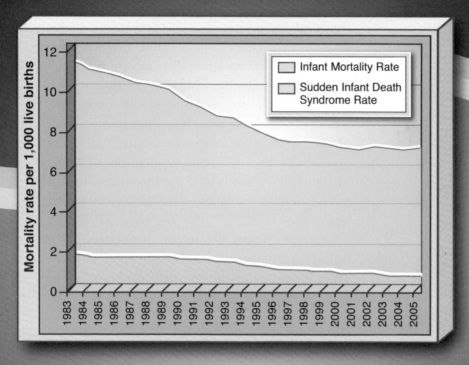

Note: *Infant mortality* includes death from age 1.

Taken from: National Sudden and Unexpected Infant/Child Death & Pregnancy Loss Resource Center, "Statistics," http://www.sidscenter.org.

increases the risk of SIDS. In any case, mothers who choose to bring their babies to bed should observe the following cautions: Soft sleep surfaces, as well as quilts, blankets, comforters or pillows should not be placed under the baby. Parents who sleep with their infants should not smoke around the baby, or use alcohol or other drugs which might make them difficult to arouse. Parents should also be aware that adult beds are not built with the same safety features as infant cribs.

Secondhand smoke. It is as important to keep the baby's environment smoke-free during infancy as it was when the mother was pregnant with the baby.

Electronic monitoring. Electronic monitors are available for use in the home. These devices sound an alarm for the parents if the child stops breathing. There is no evidence, however, that these monitors prevent SIDS. In 1986, experts consulted by the National Institutes of Health (NIH) recommended monitors only for infants at risk. These infants include those who have had one or more episodes of breath stopping; premature infants with breathing difficulties; and babies with two or more older siblings that died of SIDS. Parents who use monitors should know how to use them properly and what to for the baby if the alarm goes off.

Immunizations. There is no evidence that immunizations increase the risk of SIDS. In fact, babies who receive immunizations on schedule are less likely to die of SIDS.

How to Reduce the Risk of SIDS

Mary Best

In the following viewpoint, Mary Best discusses recommendations from the American Academy of Pediatrics (AAP) for reducing a baby's risk of dying from sudden infant death syndrome (SIDS). According to Best, doctors and researchers have learned many things about what SIDS is and what SIDS is not. For instance, Best says SIDS is not a predictable disease, but it is more likely to happen to boys. The AAP's recommendations to parents for reducing a baby's risk of dying from SIDS are based on what doctors and researchers have learned about this mysterious disease. Best lost her son Will to SIDS in 2006. She is a contributing author to the American Academy of Pediatrics' magazine *Healthy Children.*

Cloaked in mystery and superstition, SIDS has claimed the lives of babies for centuries. As medical science has advanced, scientists have ruled out a host of theories—from curses and murder to disease

SOURCE: Mary Best, "SIDS and Our Babies," *Healthy Children,* American Academy of Pediatrics, Summer 2009, pp. 12–15. Copyright American Academy of Pediatrics, 2009. Used with permission of the American Academy of Pediatrics.

To reduce risk of SIDS it has been recommended that the baby be placed on his or her back and to sleep on a safety-approved crib mattress. **(Chris Priest/ Photo Researchers, Inc.)**

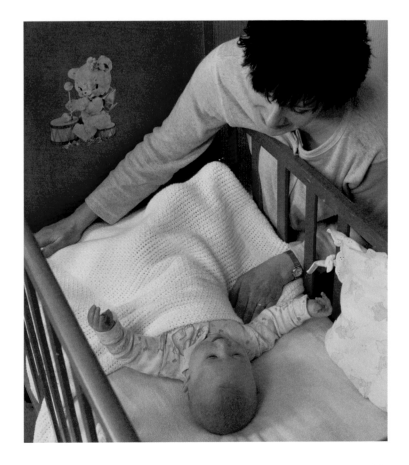

and suffocation. In 1969 the National Institutes of Health applied the term SIDS as a specific medical disease.

The reasons why a baby dies of SIDS, however, remain a diagnosis of exclusion.

"Most babies who die of SIDS appear perfectly normal," says Rachel Y. Moon, M.D., FAAP, a pediatrician at Children's National Medical Center, in Washington, D.C., and a member of the American Academy of Pediatrics' [AAP's] SIDS Task Force. "We do know that there are demographic and environmental risks," she adds, including African American and American Indian babies, infants who are born to women who smoked during pregnancy, very young women, and preterm and low birth weight infants.

"But no baby is absolutely safe from SIDS," says John Kattwinkel, M.D., FAAP, chair of the AAP's SIDS Task Force. . . .

SIDS Is . . .

- *a disease of the unknown.* SIDS is the sudden death of an infant younger than 1 year of age. The cause of death remains unexplained after a complete investigation. This includes an autopsy, examination of the death scene, a review of the infant's health, any other important medical history. The cause of death is considered a diagnosis of exclusion. SIDS is a recognized medical disorder.
- *a major cause of death.* SIDS is one of the leading causes of death for infants 1 month to 1 year of age. Most deaths occur between ages 2 and 4 months; 90 percent of SIDS deaths occur before 6 months of age. Approximately 2,500 babies in the United States die of SIDS each year— seven babies each day. SIDS claims more lives each year than AIDS, cancer, heart disease, pneumonia, muscular dystrophy, cystic fibrosis, and child abuse combined. As a result of the national Back to Sleep Campaign, launched in 1994 as a joint effort between First Candle/ SIDS Alliance, the American Academy of Pediatrics, and National Institute of Child Health and Human Development, SIDS rates have declined significantly. According to the National Center for Health Statistics, 4,890 infants died of SIDS in 1992; in 2004, 2,246 SIDS deaths were recorded in the United States.
- *also called crib death.* Most SIDS deaths occur while infants are sleeping, so the disorder is also called "crib death" or "cot death." But not all SIDS deaths occur in a baby's crib. Many have died in car seats, public places, strollers, etc. Some infants have even died in their parents' arms.
- *like a thief in the night.* Most SIDS babies appear to be healthy prior to death. A SIDS death happens quickly and silently, with no signs of suffering.

- *non-discriminatory.* While SIDS occurs in all socioeconomic, racial, and ethnic groups, African American and Native American babies are two to three times more likely to die of SIDS than Caucasian babies.
- *more harmful to boys.* 60 percent of SIDS victims are male; 40 percent are female.
- *affected by weather.* More SIDS deaths occur in the colder months.
- *devastating to parents.* Nothing can be done to save the life of a SIDS baby.

SIDS Is Not . . .
- *predictable.* There are no signs.
- *painful.* SIDS is not a cause of pain and suffering for the infant.
- *new.* SIDS has been referenced throughout Western culture, including in the Old Testament.
- *the result of Shaken Baby Syndrome or child abuse.* Experts estimate that child abuse accounts for less than 5 percent of all the SIDS cases recorded each year.
- *an ill child.* Often the only thing that can be seen medically wrong with a child prior to a SIDS death is a slight cold or the sniffles. Some babies were unusually fussy in the hours preceding their death, but these babies had no serious medical conditions, and their deaths are a shock not only to the family but also to the physicians looking after the babies.
- *contagious or infectious.*
- *hereditary.*
- *a true syndrome.* To call it a syndrome would mean it would have symptoms, and in the case of SIDS, death is the sole symptom.
- *a fatal condition of small, weak, or sickly babies.* SIDS occurs to healthy and robust babies.
- *caused by the immunizations.* Most children get their immunizations at about four months of age, which coincides with the average age of a SIDS baby. Children who

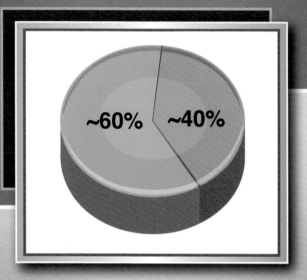

Male/Female SIDS Ratio

From 1979 to 2005, there were 62,933 males and 40,952 female SIDS deaths, according to data from the Centers for Disease Control and Prevention, for a male percentage of approximately 60 percent.

~60%   ~40%

Taken from: Compiled by editor; based on data from David T. Mage and Maria Donner, "A Unifying Theory for SIDS," *International Journal of Pediatrics*, 2009.

were never vaccinated have also died of SIDS. Deaths due to vaccine reactions or child abuse are not classified as SIDS deaths; however, this has been implicated as a possible factor in SIDS deaths.

- *caused by smothering.* If a baby was found face down or with bedclothes over the face it might be thought that smothering was the cause of death. Sometimes babies are covered with bedclothes, but others are found uncovered and free of bedclothes entirely. While it is possible for an infant to smother accidentally—and the incidence of smothering appears to be increasing—this is still somewhat rare. Not uncommonly the child is lying undisturbed as when last put to bed.
- *caused by allergies.*

• *caused by poor, bad, or uneducated parents.* SIDS happens to parents of all economic, social, educational, and racial groups. Some cultures do not report SIDS deaths or have no way to classify SIDS and this often leads some to say that there are no SIDS deaths in that area, which is misleading.

• *the cause of every unexpected infant death.*

Steps to Reduce the Risk of Sudden Infant Death

The following are recommendations from the American Academy of Pediatrics (AAP) and the National Institute for Child and Human Development (NICHD) for reducing your baby's risk of suffocating or dying from SIDS.

1. *Back is best.* Always place your baby on his or her back to sleep, for naps and at night. The back sleep position is the safest, and every sleep time counts. Side and tummy positions are unsafe.

2. *Mattress and crib safety.* Place your baby on a firm sleep surface, such as on a safety-approved crib mattress, covered by a fitted sheet.

3. *Bed behavior.* Never place your baby to sleep on pillows, quilts, sheepskins, or other soft surfaces. This includes sofas, chairs, cushions, waterbeds, etc. Also, keep soft objects, toys, and loose bedding out of your baby's sleep area. Don't use pillows, blankets, quilts, sheepskins, and pillow-like crib bumpers in your baby's sleep area, and keep any other items away from your baby's face.

4. *Bed sharing.* Keep your baby's sleep area close to, but separate from, where you and others sleep. Your baby should not sleep in a bed or on a couch or armchair with adults or other children, but he or she can sleep in the same room as you.

5. *Breast is best.* Experts recommend that mothers breastfeed through the first year of their baby's life. According to the AAP, breastfeeding is thought to help protect infants.

6. *Beat the heat.* Overheating can increase your baby's SIDS risk. To help keep your baby from overheating during sleep, dress your baby in light sleep clothing, and keep the room at a temperature that is comfortable for an adult.

7. *Smoking prohibited.* Do not allow smoking around your baby. Don't smoke before or after the birth of your baby, and don't expose your baby to secondhand smoke.

8. *Pacifier pleasers.* Research published in the *Archives of Pediatrics & Adolescent Medicine* indicates that pacifiers may help reduce the risk of SIDS. Use a clean, dry pacifier when placing your infant down to sleep, but don't force the baby to take it. If you are breastfeeding, wait until your baby is one month old before using a pacifier.

9. *Air supply.* According to another study published in the *Archives*, having a fan in the room where your baby sleeps was found to reduce the risk of SIDS by 72 percent. More research is needed to confirm these results, and fans cannot take the place of your baby sleeping on her back.

> **FAST FACT**
>
> According to the American Academy of Pediatrics, approximately 20 percent of SIDS deaths occur while an infant is under the watch of a nonparental caregiver.

10. *False confidence.* Avoid products that claim to reduce the risk of SIDS because most have not been tested for effectiveness or safety. If you have questions about using monitors for other conditions talk with your pediatrician.

11. *Tummy time.* Provide "tummy time" when your baby is awake and someone is watching—it's a good way to help baby strengthen muscles. Change the direction that your baby lies in the crib from time to time.

SIDS Is a
Complicated Disease

Margaret Renkl

Thousands of babies die every year from sudden infant death syndrome (SIDS), a complicated and difficult disease to diagnose, says Margaret Renkl in the following viewpoint. According to Renkl, scientists face difficulties in understanding why SIDS occurs because the disease is challenging to diagnose. SIDS is diagnosed only after a time-consuming investigation and generally after all other diagnoses have been ruled out. Despite the difficulties, Renkl says, researchers have found some answers about the disease. For instance, they know that putting babies to sleep on their backs lowers the risk of SIDS. Margaret Renkl is a writer whose articles have appeared in *Parenting* magazine, as well as *Good Housekeeping*, *Health*, and *Ladies' Home Journal*.

SOURCE: Margaret Renkl, "Lost Babies: Parents May Think the Back to Sleep Campaign Solved the Mystery of SIDS But Infants Are Still Dying, and Experts Are Trying to Find Out Why," *Parenting*, September 2008, pp. 118+. Copyright 2008 by Bonnier Corporation. Reproduced with permission of Bonnier Corporation via Copyright Clearance Center.

Whon Melissa and Rudy Haberzettl's son Jacob was born in November 2006, he was perfect in every way—full-term, healthy weight, and a champion eater. Like many new moms, Melissa was determined to follow doctor's orders: She breastfed Jake exclusively, put him to sleep on his back, never exposed him to cigarette smoke, and kept soft toys and bedding out of his crib. And Jake thrived. "He was such a happy baby, always looking around and cooing," remembers the Colorado Springs mom.

Of course Melissa had heard about sudden infant death syndrome (SIDS)—the designation most commonly used when a healthy baby dies in his sleep, suddenly and without any medical explanation—but she wasn't really worried about it. "When you do everything right, you just don't think it can happen to you," she says.

But when Jake was 3 months old, the unthinkable happened.

The Unthinkable

Melissa had arranged to return to work two days a week as a physical therapist, and she had chosen an in-home day-care center highly recommended by friends. Though she felt anguished about leaving her baby for the first time, she also felt certain Jake was in good hands, and she resisted the impulse to check in. Rudy, also a physical therapist, didn't. He called the sitter three times, reporting to Melissa each time that the baby was just fine. He planned to pick up Jake at 3:30 PM. Melissa hadn't heard from Rudy by 4 PM, so she called his cell. The instant she heard Rudy's voice, she knew something was wrong. "I could tell he'd been crying, and my husband does not cry." When Melissa asked, "Is Jake okay?" Rudy just said, "Stay where you are. I'm coming to get you."

Trying not to panic, Melissa called the sitter, but the person who answered would tell her only that the sitter wasn't available. By the time her husband arrived in a police cruiser a few minutes later, Melissa understood. "Jake's dead," she said as soon as Rudy stepped out of the car. "When he said yes, I just fell apart."

The death of a healthy baby is always a terrible shock, but it may be even more shocking today. That's partly because SIDS, which is classified as a natural cause of death, is considered so rare. The official rate from the National Centers for Health Statistics (NCHS) is roughly one death for every 2,000 live births—or .0005 percent. The other reason? Many parents believe that the only babies still dying of SIDS are the ones whose caregivers just aren't following the safe-sleep rules. It's hard to blame them, given that the American Academy of Pediatrics's (AAP) Back to Sleep campaign, which launched in 1994, has been credited with cutting the SIDS rate in half.

But as the Haberzettls learned so tragically, SIDS is still very much a threat, despite the accomplishments of Back to Sleep. And research suggests that the real SIDS rate may in fact be significantly higher than the official numbers indicate: Although fewer than 2,500 infant deaths this year [2008] will be classified as SIDS, an additional 2,000 seemingly healthy babies under 12 months will also die mysteriously in their sleep, according to the Centers for Disease Control and Prevention (CDC). SIDS may be a very rare event, but the news is terrifying nonetheless. No parent wants to consider the possibility of losing a child, which is why we've reached out to top experts in the field to learn what they know now—14 years into the campaign—and what more can be done to save babies.

A Difficult Diagnosis

Spotting SIDS would seem fairly straightforward, but the truth is quite the opposite. And that makes it very hard to know exactly how and why babies succumb, or why the highest rates occur in infants between 2 and 4 months old. The condition can be diagnosed only when a death has been carefully investigated—including an autopsy, a

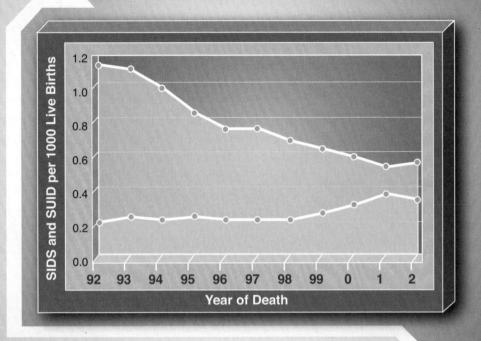

SIDS and Other Unexpected Infant Deaths, United States 1992–2002

SIDS and SUID per 1000 Live Births

1.2
1.0
0.8
0.6
0.4
0.2
0.0

92 93 94 95 96 97 98 99 0 1 2

Year of Death

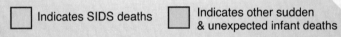

Indicates SIDS deaths

Indicates other sudden & unexpected infant deaths

Taken from: American Academy of Pediatrics Task Force on Sudden Infant Death Syndrome, "The Changing Concept of Sudden Infant Death Syndrome," *Pediatrics*, November, 2005.

study of the scene and circumstances of death, and an examination of the baby's medical history—so that all other possibilities can be ruled out. The process is expensive, and many counties don't have the resources to conduct such thorough investigations, says Amy Martin, M.D., Denver's chief medical examiner. The result? Some cases may be missed.

Government bureaucracy only compounds the problem. In 2006 the CDC acknowledged that its SIDS reporting form, which each medical examiner's office is charged with completing, was unnecessarily confusing; the revised form can be completed almost entirely by checking boxes.

But for on-the-ground forensic pathologists, says Dr. Martin, the new version is still problematic. "If you don't have enough trained investigators who can go out to the death scene, you're going to have a difficult time filling out a form like that—not to mention getting to the bottom of what really happened," she says.

And yet even when resources are available, identifying a true case of SIDS can be challenging. When a baby is found lying on her tummy—or in a bed with adults, or a crib full of soft toys—the coroner can't rule out the possibility that the baby was accidentally smothered and may call it "possible accidental asphyxia" or "threats to breathing" rather than SIDS. That's why some states today report no SIDS deaths at all, despite the fact that babies still die there every year, says Fern R. Hauck, M.D., associate professor of family medicine and public health sciences at the University of Virginia.

As Melissa Haberzettl found out, this variation in labeling—a phenomenon called code-shifting—can happen if the examiner discovers a possibly unrelated underlying condition as well. Five weeks after offering a preliminary assessment that Jake had died of SIDS, the Colorado Springs coroner changed his diagnosis. Even though the baby showed no signs of illness, the medical examiner concluded that Jake had died of viral pneumonia. "I kept asking, 'How can a healthy baby die of pneumonia?' but I never got a straight answer," says Melissa.

She sought out a second opinion from Henry Krous, M.D., a SIDS researcher at Rady Children's Hospital in San Diego. In his view, the local examiner had missed a perfectly obvious case of SIDS: "With viral pneumonia, infants don't die suddenly without getting sick first, says Dr. Krous. "If one has a degree of pneumonia that can be seen only with a microscope, and then the infant dies, he dies with it, not of it."

FAST FACT

According to the US Centers for Disease Control and Prevention, SIDS is the leading cause of death among infants aged one–twelve months and is the third leading cause overall of infant mortality in the United States.

Regardless of how or why it happens, code-shifting helps to explain why SIDS deaths have dropped in the past 14 years while other sudden infant deaths, like those attributed to accidental suffocation or even, simply, undefined causes, have increased significantly. If true SIDS cases are being assigned a wide variety of other diagnoses, it makes it nearly impossible for researchers to get a good handle on what's happening with the rates and risk factors right now, says Dr. Hauck. That's why for parents, it's more important than ever to follow the safe-sleep recommendations, including putting babies down on their backs, says Dr. Krous. "Nothing we know at the present time will absolutely prevent SIDS, but the risk can be substantially reduced."

What Is Known So Far

Despite the challenges, SIDS research goes on. And though much remains to be learned, scientists do have some answers. For instance, they know that certain infants, such as African-American, Native American, and premature babies, are at particular risk, and that certain situations (including sleeping on a soft surface and exposure to secondhand smoke) raise the odds for all babies. They also know that babies who sleep on their stomachs or sides face the biggest danger: They have twice the risk of dying from SIDS as babies who sleep on their backs. When a baby's face is turned toward the bedding, he's in a position to re-breathe the carbon dioxide he exhales, which limits the amount of oxygen he takes in. "When they aren't getting enough oxygen, most babies will do something to change their environment—they'll turn their heads, or they'll sigh, or they'll yawn," says Rachel Moon, M.D., an associate professor of pediatrics at George Washington University School of Medicine in Washington, DC. "But babies who die of SIDS don't wake up when they get into trouble, and we don't fully understand why."

One of the most plausible theories may be a brain-stem abnormality that affects the brain's ability to make and use serotonin—a theory corroborated by a new Italian study that found that serotonin overproduction caused SIDS-like deaths in mice—and it may be responsible for well over half of all cases. Along with its role affecting mood, serotonin helps regulate breathing and arousal. If that arousal center isn't functioning properly, a baby sleeping in a position that limits his oxygen may not wake up in time. This discovery, made by researchers at Children's Hospital Boston, helps explain why SIDS rates drop dramatically after 6 months and disappear entirely at one year: The brain stem continues to mature, and even abnormal brain stems are eventually able to process serotonin appropriately.

The Many Sides of SIDS

As encouraging as this research is, it's become increasingly clear that the syndrome likely has several biological explanations, with different babies dying for different physiological reasons—and that complicates the mystery even more. Along with brain-stem problems, researchers are also looking into undiagnosed genetic anomalies that cause no symptoms but are ultimately fatal. A metabolic disorder called MCADD (medium chain acyl-CoA dehydrogenase deficiency), for instance, impairs the baby's ability to process fatty acids, eventually causing a sudden and fatal interruption in heart function. Another condition is long QT syndrome, an electrical disorder in the heart that causes sudden bursts of extremely rapid heartbeats and can lead to cardiac arrest. MCADD and long QT syndrome account for fewer than 15 percent of SIDS cases, but both disorders can be successfully treated if caught in time by a blood test; unfortunately, these tests aren't routine in most states.

Although some infants seem to be at greater genetic risk for SIDS, it's also possible that all babies are susceptible if the factors are strong enough at the time of greatest vulnerability. "It probably takes more of a stressor to tip a baby who has no predisposition over into SIDS than it takes for a genetically susceptible baby, but it could still happen," says Dr. Moon.

Preliminary research also suggests that babies who begin daycare before 4 months of age, like Jake Haberzettl, may be at increased risk as well. In the most recent AAP analysis, about 20 percent of all SIDS deaths occurred while the baby was in the care of someone other than a parent. One third of the infants died during the first week of childcare, and half those deaths occurred on the very first day. "It may be that starting a new routine interrupts the baby's sleep cycle, so that when he finally does fall asleep, he sleeps too deeply," says Dr. Moon. It may also be that some providers don't recognize the risks of tummy sleeping. The danger? Babies who are accustomed to sleeping on their backs are 18 times more likely to die from SIDS

SIDS can only be diagnosed after a time-consuming investigation that rules out all other possible diagnoses. (© **Science Faction/Superstock**)

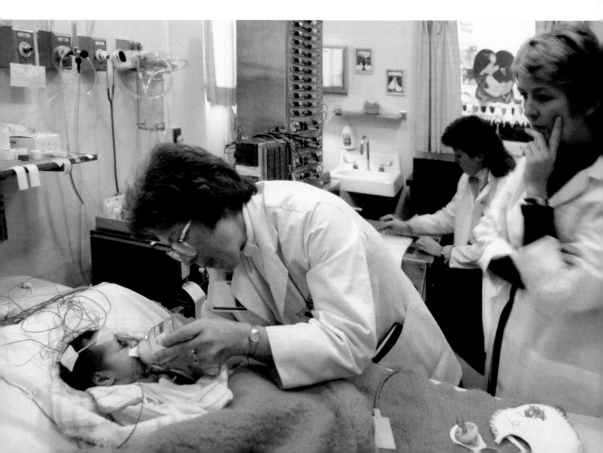

when put down to sleep on their stomachs. That's why it's important for parents to emphasize safe-sleeping practices with their providers, and try to use only a licensed facility.

Eventually, researchers hope that it will be possible to create a diagnostic test to identify the babies most at risk for SIDS. "But our real dream is to develop some sort of protection to use through the risk period," says Dr. Krous. Reaching that goal will take a lot more funding, a lot more research, and more accurate information from death-scene investigations. As Dr. Krous says, "That's a long way off, but that's the dream. To save lives."

Melissa Haberzettl shares this dream. In March [2008], she gave birth to a second son, Dylan Jacob, whose middle name is a tribute to the older brother he'll never know. "I was nervous about trying to get pregnant again," says Melissa, "but Rudy and I both said to ourselves, 'We have to try.'" (To make sure his risk was low, Dylan was tested for both MCADD and long QT syndrome, but he has neither.) And she continues to keep up with SIDS research. "I'm hopeful that in my lifetime, people will say, 'SIDS? What's that?' And no other family will have to go through what we did when Jake died."

Low Serotonin Levels May Cause SIDS

Children's Hospital Boston

In the following viewpoint, doctors at Children's Hospital Boston discuss research findings that suggest that low levels of serotonin in the brain stem may be a cause of sudden infant death syndrome (SIDS). The brain stem controls primitive yet essential functions of the body, such as breathing and circulating blood. Serotonin is a brain chemical that transmits signals between nerve cells and whose levels are important for many brain functions, such as mood regulation. Researchers at Children's Hospital Boston analyzed tissue samples from babies who died from SIDS as well as babies who died from other causes. The researchers found that serotonin levels in the brain stems of babies who died from SIDS were significantly lower than the levels in the babies who died of other causes. The researchers hypothesize that infants with low amounts of brain stem serotonin cannot rouse themselves from sleep when stressful moments such as low oxygen levels are experienced. The researchers' findings are published in the *Journal of the American Medical Association.* Children's Hospital Boston is the primary pediatric teaching hospital of Harvard Medical School.

SOURCE: Jhodie R. Duncan, PhD, David S. Paterson, PhD, Jill M. Hoffman, BS, David J. Mokler, PhD, Natalia S. Borenstein, MS, Richard A. Belliveau, BA, Henry F. Krous, MD, Elisabeth A. Haas, BA, Christina Stanley, MD, Eugene E. Nattie, MD, Felicia L. Trachtenberg, PhD, Hannah C. Kinney, MD, "Brainstem Serotonergic Deficiency in Sudden Infant Brain Syndrome," *JAMA,* vol. 303, no. 5, February 3, 2010. Copyright © 2010 by American Medical Association. All rights reserved. Reproduced by permission.

Taking the next step in more than 20 years of research, researchers at Children's Hospital Boston have linked sudden infant death syndrome (SIDS) with low production of serotonin in the brainstem, based on a comparison of brainstem samples from infants dying of SIDS compared to brainstems of infants dying from other, known causes.

The findings, published in the Feb. 3 [2010] issue of *The Journal of the American Medical Association*, may give a concrete approach to identifying babies at risk for SIDS, the leading cause of death for infants between 1 and 12 months old in the United States.

Brainstem Levels of Serotonin

In the brainstem, serotonin helps regulate some of the body's involuntary actions, such as breathing, heart rate and blood pressure during sleep. The researchers, led by Children's neuropathologist Hannah Kinney, believe that a low serotonin level impairs the function of the brainstem circuits that regulate these activities, putting a baby at risk for sudden death from stresses such as rebreathing carbon dioxide when sleeping in the face down position.

The future goal of this work is to devise a test to identify infants with a serotonin brainstem defect early, and to develop preventive treatments that would correct the serotonin deficiency.

In 2006, Kinney and colleagues showed that SIDS is associated with abnormalities in the number of cells and receptors related to serotonin in the brainstem, but it wasn't clear whether SIDS may be caused by overproduction or underproduction of the chemical.

In the new study, the team measured the levels of serotonin and tryptophan hydroxylase, the enzyme that helps make serotonin, in 35 infants dying from SIDS and two control groups (5 infants dying acutely from other causes,

> **FAST FACT**
>
> According to death statistics from the US Centers for Disease Control and Prevention, six infants die from SIDS every day in the United States.

and 5 hospitalized infants with chronic hypoxia-ischemia (insufficient oxygen supply to tissues). Tissue samples from the brainstem were obtained from autopsies and provided by research partners at the San Diego County Medical Examiner's Office in California.

Lower Serotonin Levels in SIDS Babies

Compared with controls, the serotonin levels in the lower brainstem were 26 percent lower in the SIDS cases, while the tryptophan hydroxylase levels were 22 percent lower.

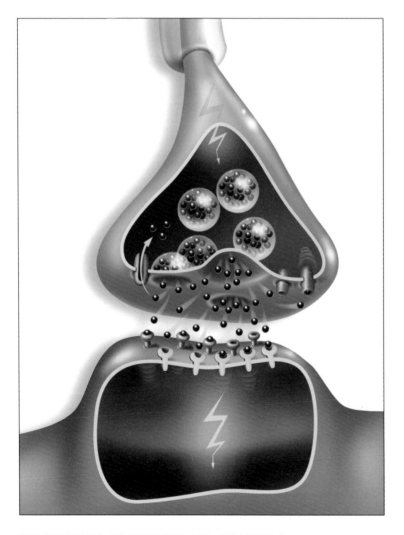

This illustration shows a serotoninergic synapse. A nerve impulse is transmitted between two synapses by serotonin (maroon balls). Researchers think there may be a link between SIDS and low production of serotonin in the brain stems of babies. **(BSIP/Photo Researchers, Inc.)**

Levels of binding to serotonin receptors were also lower by more than 50 percent. The consistency and correlation of these findings with each other reinforce the idea that SIDS in the majority of cases is a disorder of serotonin [in the] the brainstem, the researchers say.

"The baby looks normal during the day; there's nothing that would tell you that baby is going to die of SIDS that night," says Kinney, who has studied SIDS for more than 20 years. "There's something about sleep that unmasks the defect, which we believe is in serotonin circuits: the baby experiences some kind of stress during sleep, such as rebreathing carbon dioxide in the face-down position or

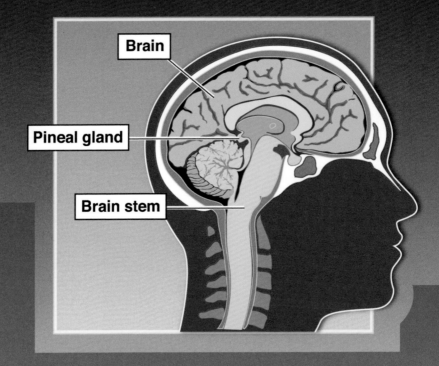

Low Levels of Serotonin in Brain Stem Implicated as Likely Cause of SIDS

Brain

Pineal gland

Brain stem

Taken from: Beliefnet.com, "Dysthymia," 2006. http://www.beliefnet.com.

increased temperature from overbundling, that cannot be compensated for by the defective brainstem circuits, and the baby then goes on to die."

In a normal baby rebreathing carbon dioxide, serotonin pathways in the brainstem would stir the baby awake long enough to turn its head, allowing it to breathe fresh air, Kinney adds. A baby with low serotonin levels in the brainstem may never stir.

SIDS has puzzled doctors and families for decades, but once the medical community recognized that a baby's position while sleeping affects the risk for SIDS, national awareness campaigns sprouted to persuade parents to place babies to sleep on their backs. However, such campaigns haven't completely solved the problem, prompting ongoing research to find a biological component to SIDS.

While this study provides strong evidence for a biological cause of SIDS, it also shows that other risk factors, such as sleeping on one's stomach, can aggravate the risk. Of the SIDS infants in the current study, 95 percent died with at least one risk factor, and 88 percent died with at least two.

The next step in this research is to find out what causes abnormally low serotonin levels in the first place. Genetic variations may be partly responsible, says neuroscientist David Paterson, in Kinney's lab, a contributing author of the paper. Kinney's lab is searching for such variations.

The Search for a Genetic Cause of SIDS

Vita Lerman

Researchers analyzing tissues from SIDS (sudden infant death syndrome) babies have found several mutations in genes that are important in the autonomic nervous system (ANS) and in the production of the brain chemical serotonin, says Vita Lerman in the following viewpoint. According to Lerman, the research team, led by Debra Weese-Mayer from Children's Memorial Hospital in Chicago, looked at serotonin and ANS genes because previous studies had suggested that SIDS may be caused by problems in the ANS and/or by defective serotonin networks. Lerman says the researchers are encouraged by their findings, but they stress that more research is needed in order to fully understand the genetics behind SIDS. Vita Lerman is a medical writer and editor for the *Child's Doctor*, a publication of Children's Memorial Hospital.

The widespread "Back to Sleep" and "Back Is Best" campaigns to prevent sudden infant death syndrome (SIDS) by placing babies to sleep on their backs and heeding other modifiable risk factors for SIDS successfully reduced the number of unexplained infant deaths, but not completely. More than 2,000 infants still succumb to SIDS in the United States each year, more often in African American families, even when parents did everything right. Because so many parents followed recommendations, yet babies were still dying, researchers turned to genetics.

Now a decade later, a genetic picture of SIDS susceptibility is starting to emerge. One of the major researchers determined to find the missing pieces within this genetic puzzle is Debra E. Weese-Mayer, MD, who leads the Center for Autonomic Medicine in Pediatrics (CAMP) at [Chicago's] Children's Memorial Hospital.

"Once we define the genetic profile of SIDS susceptibility, a pharmacological intervention that targets the underlying mechanism could be a possibility," says Weese-Mayer. "We would also be able to identify high-risk infants through newborn screening or prenatal testing, and offer genetic testing to families to estimate risk."

FAST FACT

According to the US Department of Health and Human Services, the rate of death from SIDS for African Americans was nearly double that of non-Hispanic whites in 2006.

SIDS, Serotonin, and the Autonomic Nervous System

Studies suggest that there might be different mechanisms accounting for the end result of sudden unexplained deaths, with bases in varied but potentially integrated systems. Weese-Mayer's search for SIDS-related candidate genes has focused on the serotonin network, the autonomic nervous system [ANS], and their interrelationships.

"These are very promising directions for research," says Weese-Mayer. "Altered function and development of

Genetic Mutations Associated with SIDS

Presence of mutations in autonomic nervous system genes; based on a study of 92 SIDS babies and 92 healthy babies.

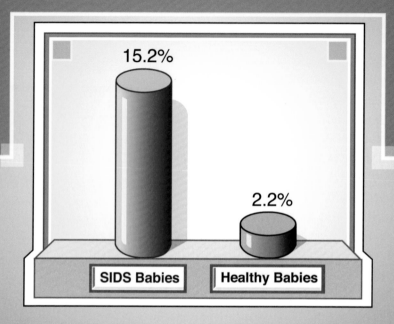

15.2%

2.2%

SIDS Babies   Healthy Babies

Taken from: Compiled by editor; based on data from Debra Weese-Mayer, et. al, "Sudden Infant Death Syndrome: Case-Control Frequency Differences at Genes Pertinent to Early Autonomic Nervous System Embryologic Development," *Pediatric Research*, September 2004.

the serotonin system in SIDS cases have been established in neuropathological studies. Our team is trying to identify the specific genetic variants responsible for these changes," she explains.

Also, from clinical data collected before death, we know that there is a relationship between SIDS and problems in the ANS. Further, we know that serotonin influences regulation of breathing, heart rate, body temperature and the sleep-wake cycle, and is integral to the ANS.

So dysregulation of these autonomic processes in SIDS might be caused by genetic variants within the serotonin network. Or, SIDS susceptibility might be a result of genetic variants within both the ANS and the serotonin system or in the genes regulating the interconnected mechanisms between these systems.

Serotonin Transporter Gene Variations

To date, Weese-Mayer's team has contributed important pieces to the SIDS puzzle, especially with respect to the role of the serotonin transporter gene *(5-HTT)*, which is a single protein that globally regulates serotonin re-uptake. Her research has established strong associations between SIDS and certain variations in the *5-HTT* gene that might explain the neuroanatomic findings in SIDS.

Specifically, Weese-Mayer's team has shown that the long allele [version] of the *5-HTT* gene promoter region and the 12 repeat allele . . . of the *5-HTT* gene appear together more frequently in African American SIDS cases. Yet the long allele of the *5-HTT* gene promoter region, alone, is more prevalent among Caucasian infants who have died from SIDS.

"These polymorphisms [variations] in the serotonin transporter gene may play an important role in SIDS susceptibility and may begin to explain the ethnic differences in SIDS risk," says Weese-Mayer.

> These findings also imply that the resultant change in serotonin levels may contribute to SIDS risk. Or, these polymorphisms may relate to SIDS risk through a developmental effect on . . . [brainstem] neurons, which release serotonin in the brainstem in early embryology [the first stages of prenatal development]. In fact, new findings from our collaborators in Italy suggest that the serotonin transporter promoter long allele combined with morphological [biological form] developmental defects of the . . . [brainstem neurons] predispose infants to SIDS.

PHOX2B Gene in SIDS

Weese-Mayer's research also found that several distinct variations in the *PHOX2B* gene are more common in SIDS cases. . . . Earlier she and colleagues established *PHOX2B* as the disease-defining gene for congenital central hypoventilation syndrome (CCHS), a key disorder of ANS dysregulation. Weese-Mayer's team also identified an increased incidence of SIDS in CCHS families, which led to more intensive scrutiny of *PHOX2B*. Her team discovered that specific mutations in other genes important in early embryology of the ANS may contribute some SIDS risk as well. As she explains, "Our underlying premise is that SIDS and CCHS are related within the rubric [list of criteria] of disorders of ANS dysregulation."

Polarized light micrograph of serotonin (5-HTT). Research has established a strong association between SIDS and variations of the 5-HTT gene. (Michael W. Davidson/ Photo Researchers, Inc.)

Tissue Donations Needed

Although researchers are advancing in the search to understand how the puzzle pieces fit together, the definitive SIDS gene or a set pattern of closely related genetic variants responsible for SIDS remains elusive. Weese-Mayer and her team are determined to reveal the genetic profile of SIDS through their relentless inquiry. Critical to this search are the tissue samples from SIDS cases, which she receives from the National Institute of Child Health and Human Development–funded University of Maryland Brain and Tissue Bank. "By contributing to a central repository for rare diseases, parents can be assured that they and their loved ones are helping to advance science and unlock the mystery that took away the precious life of their child. Donating to the bank is truly the gift of a lifetime," says Weese-Mayer.

CHAPTER 2

Controversies Surrounding SIDS

Toxic Gases in Crib Mattresses Are to Blame for SIDS

Jane Sheppard

In the following viewpoint, Jane Sheppard argues that crib mattresses are releasing toxic gases that are poisoning babies and are a likely cause of sudden infant death syndrome (SIDS). According to Sheppard, crib mattresses contain antimony (a metal used in flame retardants) and many other toxic substances that babies should not be exposed to. She maintains that SIDS deaths, or crib deaths, as they are often called, have decreased in New Zealand since that country began a campaign to wrap mattresses in a cover that blocks the release of the gases. Jane Sheppard is the founder of Healthy Child, a company that sells environmentally safe and nontoxic child-care products and is an advocate of holistic and natural medicine.

Have you heard about toxic gases in crib mattresses causing SIDS or crib death? Basically, the theory is that toxic gases are generated from chemicals in a baby's crib mattress. If a baby breathes or absorbs a lethal dose of the gases, the central nervous

Photo on facing page. Researchers have found a link between SIDS and babies who died while sleeping with their parents in bed or on a sofa. (© **Picture Partners/ Alamy**)

system shuts down, stopping breathing and then heart function. These gases can fatally poison a baby, without waking the sleeping baby.

There is a cot (crib) death prevention campaign in New Zealand [NZ] to wrap crib mattresses in a cover that blocks the gases from getting to the babies. This has been going on for the past 11 years [since the late 1990s].

I was shocked when I first heard about it 10 years ago and did a lot of checking to find out what was really going on. I contacted Dr. James Sprott, one of the main scientists publishing this theory, and I have been in touch with

A toddler stands on an all-organic mattress that is free from chemicals found in most mattresses. Researchers say there is a link between SIDS and mattress outgassing. (Gerald Martineau/Washington Post/Getty Images)

him and other environmental scientists and continue to follow the results of the NZ crib death (SIDS) prevention campaign. . . .

The Toxic Gas Explanation

Has this been scientifically proven? No, it has not. Nor has it been disproven. We definitely need more research. But when you look at the evidence we do have, it's very compelling and it makes complete sense. It even logically explains every factor already known about crib death.

What is so compelling to me is that there have been no SIDS deaths among the large number of babies in New Zealand who have slept on correctly wrapped mattresses designed to block the gases. This is quite a crucial piece of information for parents. It's the only crib death prevention advice that has ever been 100% successful! If you've read elsewhere that some babies have been found to die on wrapped mattresses, this has never been substantiated and is just not true.

> **FAST FACT**
>
> The SIDS death rate in New Zealand in 2004 was 0.8 deaths per one thousand live births. This was the lowest rate since SIDS became classified as a separate category of death, according to the World Health Organization.

Why haven't you heard about this in the news or from your doctor? Is there more research being done on this issue? No, there is not, because [the US] government and most SIDS organizations have essentially closed the book on the toxic gas explanation. Several SIDS organizations came up with a position paper on the issue in 2004 and that's what most doctors and media go by. This position paper says there is insufficient evidence to support the claims and that parents should disregard the toxic gas information. So don't hold your breath on additional research on this issue.

What do these SIDS organizations mostly base their conclusions on? A faulty report published in 1998 that was commissioned by the British government, under Lady Limerick. But the 1998 UK Limerick Report did not disprove the toxic gas theory for cot death (crib death). In fact, Dr. Sprott says the Limerick Committee's research proved the gas generation on which the toxic gas theory is based. . . .

In addition, they focused on antimony [a metallic element] and ignored the other numerous chemicals in mattresses that can be toxic to babies. Worse yet in this position paper, First Candle/SIDS Alliance tells parents to continue to use vinyl covered crib mattresses! This is terrible advice—we know that vinyl (PVC) is dangerous for babies. I do understand their concern that parents trying to avoid exposure may put their babies to sleep on surfaces other than a firm, flat mattress. But there are now nontoxic, safe, firm, flat organic baby crib mattresses available that are much safer than vinyl.

So with little hope of further research, we're left on our own to figure out if we should take action or not.

Toxic Crib Matresses

Here's my take on this issue after paying close attention and following this for over 10 years:

I believe some babies are dying from toxic poisoning in their cribs. I don't think it's the only cause of SIDS since it's also known that vaccinations have caused baby deaths that have been labeled as SIDS. Most likely, in my opinion, it's a combination of the two. There could be other causes, but I do believe it's mostly a toxicity issue. There may even be some underlying medical condition, as some studies suggest, that is triggered by an environmental toxic assault.

The toxic gas issue may not be exactly as explained by Dr. Sprott. But even if it turns out that the toxic gases generated from antimony, arsenic and phosphorus are not an issue in crib death, the fact remains that typical crib mattresses do contain poisons and babies should not be sleeping on polyurethane foam covered in vinyl and loaded with fire retardants, chemical plasticizers and biocides. It's a known

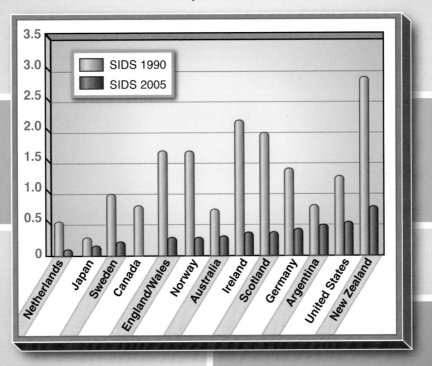

SIDS Death Rates Around the World

SIDS Deaths per 1,000 live births

Legend:
- SIDS 1990
- SIDS 2005

Countries (x-axis): Netherlands, Japan, Sweden, Canada, England/Wales, Norway, Australia, Ireland, Scotland, Germany, Argentina, United States, New Zealand

Taken from: National Sudden and Unexpected Infant/Child Death & Pregnancy Loss Resource Center, http://www.sidscenter.org.

fact that chemical plasticizers, such as phthalates, leach out of vinyl mattress covers. Additionally, toxic fire retardants can leach out into the air. We also know for a fact that cribs are off-gassing formaldehyde and other [volatile organic compounds]. Toxic crib and mattress materials are known to cause neurological, respiratory, reproductive or immune problems in infants. Small, developing babies should not be breathing in these chemicals and gases as they sleep!

The bottom line is that babies should not be sleeping on crib mattresses that contain any toxic materials during their most vulnerable period of brain and immune development.

Toxic Gases in Crib Mattresses Do Not Cause SIDS

First Candle

First Candle, previously the SIDS Alliance, is a nonprofit organization dedicated to eliminating sudden infant death syndrome (SIDS) and keeping babies safe during their first year of life. In the following viewpoint, First Candle asserts that available scientific evidence refutes the toxic gas theory from crib mattresses as a cause of SIDS. According to First Candle, there is no link between the occurrence of SIDS deaths and the addition of antimony, an ingredient in flame retardants, to crib mattresses. Babies die of SIDS on mattresses that do not contain antimony and babies die of SIDS on mattresses designed to prevent toxic gases from escaping. First Candle maintains that the best way to prevent SIDS from occurring is to place babies on their backs to sleep.

First Candle/SIDS Alliance has carefully followed and reviewed all studies that have been done to try and substantiate the toxic gas hypothesis but, in short, there has been no real evidence to support the claims. . . . Organizations and researchers from around

SOURCE: "Toxic Gas Theory, Mattresses and SIDS," firstcandle .org, July, 2009. Copyright © 2009 by First Candle/SIDS Alliance. Reproduced by permission.

the world share our position. Even experts in New Zealand, where this theory originated, do not support the claims.

Following are some of the main points of the follow-up studies done abroad to support our position here in the United States:

- There is no difference in antimony [a metallic element] in babies that die of cot death/SIDS and other babies;
- Antimony is found in most babies, even before birth (before they could have had any exposure to mattresses). It could come from maternal diet, but antimony is everywhere, including common household dust.
- No antimony was added to mattresses before 1988, and yet SIDS deaths were occurring pre-1988 at the rate of about 2,000 per year (now less than 500 per year).

First Candle, a non-profit group battling SIDS, says the best way to prevent SIDS from occurring is to place babies to sleep on their backs. (© Ilja Dubovskis/Alamy)

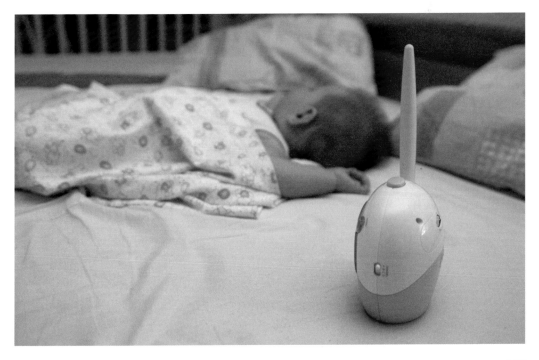

Estimated Health Risks for Children of Flame-Retardant Chemicals in Mattresses

Average Daily Dose (ADD) and Acceptable Daily Intake (ADI) are based on milligrams per kilograms per day for a child 5 years old. Younger children were not considered. Table shows that ADD from mattresses are less than ADI, so mattresses should be safe.

	Boric Acid	Antimony Trioxide	Decabromo-diphenyl Oxide
ADD Total (Average Daily Dose)	0.005	0.026	0.002
ADI (Acceptable Daily Intake)	0.10	2.3	3.2
Hazard Index, HI (Numbers less than one are considered safe)	0.05	0.01	0.001

Taken from: US Consumer Product Safety Commission, "Quantitative Assessment."

• The year after antimony was first added to mattresses, 1989, was the year that cot deaths began to decrease—at first a small decrease and then, after 1991 following campaigns to sleep babies on the back, a rapid decrease—cot deaths dropped in all by over 70% between 1988 and 1995.

• The theory claims that the decrease was due to publicizing advice to wrap mattresses is unfounded: as of 1993–1995, only 2% of babies were sleeping on wrapped mattresses; babies have also been found to die on wrapped mattresses.

- Cot death occurs in countries where no antimony has been added to mattresses.
- When comparing babies who die and babies who live, proportionately more of the babies who live sleep on PVC [polyvinyl chloride] mattresses.
- According to the theory, death occurs because the toxic gas reduces acetylcholinesterase [an enzyme that breaks down the brain chemical acetylcholine], leading to heart failure, but post mortem examinations of babies who die show no reduction in acetylcholinesterase.
- The fungus *Scopulariopsis brevicaulis* that was said to be present on all cot mattresses and which was essential for the release of toxic gases, is actually hardly ever present on cot mattresses.

Insufficient Evidence

In summary, to date, there is insufficient scientific evidence to support the claim that toxic fumes resulting from a chemical reaction between bedwetting and a flame retardant chemical used in infant mattresses (antimony) are a cause of SIDS. According to experts both in the U.S. and abroad, the mattress wrapping process proposed by proponents of this theory will not aid in preventing a SIDS death. We encourage parents to avoid old and worn mattresses, especially those that may have foam or padding exposed (increasing the potential for bacteria) or those . . . where indentations are made when your hand is placed firmly on the surface.

The majority of mattresses that have been sold in the United States for many years provide a vinyl or other protective covering for the mattress. By purchasing/using this type of mattress (as firm as possible) covering it with only a sheet, and placing your baby to sleep on its back, you will be providing the greatest protection for your sleeping baby.

> **FAST FACT**
>
> The US Consumer Product Safety Commission began requiring that mattresses (including crib mattresses) meet flammability standards in 1973.

The Back to Sleep Campaign Has Been Successful

National Institute of Child Health and Human Development

In the following viewpoint the National Institute of Child Health and Human Development (NICHD) asserts that the Back to Sleep campaign successfully lowered the rate of sudden infant death syndrome (SIDS) deaths in the United States. In 1974 the US Congress tasked the NICHD with educating the public about sudden infant death syndrome and lowering the number of SIDS deaths in the United States. In 1994, after research showed that back sleeping could prevent SIDS deaths, the NICHD and the American Academy of Pediatrics created the Back to Sleep campaign to encourage parents and other caregivers to place babies to sleep on their backs. The NICHD says it is constantly modifying and improving the Back to Sleep message, because putting babies to sleep on their backs is still one of the best ways to prevent SIDS. The NICHD is one of twenty-seven centers and institutes in the National Institutes of Health, the nation's premier medical research agency.

SOURCE: "Sudden Infant Death Syndrome (SIDS) Awareness Month: Highlights of NICHD Outreach," National Institute of Child Health and Human Development, October 21, 2010.

SIDS is the sudden, unexplained death of an infant younger than one year of age. It is the leading cause of death in children between one month and one year of age. In 2006, more than 2,300 infants died of SIDS in the United States.

The NICHD [National Institute of Child Health & Human Development] Spotlights for October—SIDS Awareness Month—highlight the Institute's activities related to SIDS. The first one [was titled] Timely Advice on Safe Infant Sleep: Research on Sudden Infant Death Syndrome (SIDS) and described the NICHD's research efforts and findings related to SIDS. The NICHD's portfolio on SIDS also includes outreach—involving communities in reducing SIDS risk. This Spotlight describes the Institute's activities related to SIDS education and risk-reduction activities, part of its multifaceted approach to understanding SIDS and eliminating it worldwide.

Beginning of the Back to Sleep Campaign

The NICHD has been conducting and supporting research to understand SIDS for many decades. In 1974, Congress passed the Sudden Infant Death Syndrome Act (Public Law 93-270), which not only placed the NICHD at the forefront of SIDS research, but also charged the NICHD with providing information to the public about SIDS and ways to reduce the risk of SIDS.

In 1994, the NICHD, the American Academy of Pediatrics (AAP), and other partners established a public health campaign to educate parents, caregivers, and health care providers about ways to reduce the risk of SIDS. At the time, research from the NICHD and other sources revealed that healthy babies should be placed on their backs or sides to sleep to reduce the risk of SIDS. From these research findings, "back to sleep" became the main message

> **FAST FACT**
>
> In 2009 less than 12 percent of parents placed their babies to sleep on their stomachs, according to the National Infant Sleep Position Survey.

In response to the Back to Sleep campaign many manufacturers produced products, like this one called Baby Sleep Safe, that assure the baby will sleep on its back. (AP Images/PRNewsFoto/ BabySleepsSafe)

and name of the campaign. The message was further refined in 1996, when findings from NICHD-supported and other research led the AAP to revise its recommendation to say that healthy babies should sleep wholly on their backs as the best way to reduce the risk of SIDS.

In 1993, before the Back to Sleep campaign began, the U.S. SIDS rate was 1.17 deaths for each 1,000 live births. By 2000, the U.S. SIDS rate [had] decreased by about 50 percent to 0.62 for each 1,000 live births and has continued to decline. Although thousands of infants have not succumbed to SIDS, babies are still dying of SIDS, and rates in certain populations are much higher than the national average.

The NICHD's goal is ultimately to eliminate SIDS deaths, both in the United States and worldwide. To do so, the Back to Sleep campaign and the NICHD continue reaching out to various communities with safe sleep messages. . . .

Tailoring the Message

Using studies of health education and of SIDS outreach, campaign leaders discovered that response to safe sleep messages differs among different communities and ethnicities. To reach as many people with safe sleep messages as possible, the campaign has created several outreach efforts tailored to different audiences. For example:

• Back to Sleep began offering materials in Spanish very early in the campaign's existence and provides a variety of Spanish materials today to help spread safe sleep messages to Spanish-speaking communities.

• In 2000, the NICHD and its Back to Sleep partners worked with national African American organizations to design materials about SIDS for African American families and communities.

  • In addition to a suite of materials focused on reaching African Americans, the NICHD also partnered with the Alpha Kappa Alpha Sorority, the Women in the National Association for the Advancement of Colored People (NAACP), and the National Coalition of 100 Black Women to hold outreach summits in different parts of the country. The summits focused on training members of these organizations on ways to spread safe sleep messages in their communities.

  • These groups also collaborated on a series of radio Public Service Announcements (PSAs) that ran nationwide on the RadioOne network and printed PSAs that were placed on mass transit venues in the Washington, D.C., area.

• In 2006, the NICHD began the Mississippi SIDS African American Outreach Project to expand and improve coordination and delivery of SIDS risk-reduction information to pregnant and parenting women, their families, and other caregivers of infants younger than one year of age in the state of Mississippi. The project partners include the Mississippi Department of Health, local organizations, churches, and community groups that promote the use of culturally tailored SIDS risk-reduction materials developed by the NICHD for African American communities.

- To date [October 2010] more than 80 mini-grants have been awarded to community- and faith-based organizations to implement SIDS risk-reduction activities.

- Train-the-trainer sessions are also conducted for those who provide health and support services in all nine health districts across Mississippi.

- In 2003–2004, the NICHD began working with representatives from American Indian/Alaska Native (AI/AN) communities to understand the unique information needs of these communities. As a result, in 2009, the NICHD and its AI/AN partners released safe sleep materials tailored for AI/ANs. . . .

- Health care providers have been a primary audience for information about ways to reduce the risk of SIDS since the campaign started but, early on, this outreach focused mostly on doctors.

  - Research showed that parents are more likely to follow safe sleep practices if they see those practices modeled by nurses and other nursery staff. So in 2007, in collaboration with the National Institute on Nursing Research and other national organizations, the NICHD launched the printed Continuing Education Module on SIDS Risk Reduction: Curriculum for Nurses to help nurses take advantage of their unique position as trusted advisors to parents and families. . . .

  - The NICHD is currently working in partnership with several national pharmacist organizations and other groups to create a similar printed module on SIDS risk reduction for pharmacists.

• In addition, the campaign continues to provide materials for health care providers in general.

New Trends in Outreach

Back to Sleep outreach no longer relies solely on in-person distribution of printed materials. Although the campaign still provides printed materials, it also uses various media formats to reach various audiences. For example:

• In 2010, the NICHD, the National Institute on Nursing Research, and other national organizations, launched the online Continuing Education Program on SIDS Risk Reduction: Curriculum for Nurses as a complement to the printed version. Both the printed and online modules provide a quick and portable way for nurses to learn about SIDS and how to educate parents and caregivers about reducing SIDS risk. . . .

• Later in 2010, the NICHD will launch a similar online continuing education module on SIDS risk reduction for pharmacists.

• Among the additional materials for outreach to AI/AN communities is the Healthy Native Babies Project Toolkit—an interactive CD-ROM that will allow health workers and other outreach personnel to tailor materials to specific Tribal areas and Tribes using photos, language, and other graphic elements specific to those Tribes. The Toolkit provides flexibility for creating outreach materials that are culturally tailored to different AI/AN Tribes.

• The NICHD will also be working with its AI/AN partners to create an online self-study module on SIDS risk reduction that will allow community health and outreach workers even in rural areas to have access to the latest information on SIDS risk reduction.

• The NICHD is in the process of revamping the Back to Sleep Web site to make it more comprehensive and more interactive. Plans for the site include an interactive "game" to help parents and caregivers learn how to make a safe sleep environment for their babies. . . .

• The NICHD also took part in the text4baby program—a free service that delivers evidence-based health information about pregnancy and baby's first year directly to the mobile devices of moms-to-be and new moms. Those interested can opt-in to this public-private partnership between the National Healthy Mothers Healthy Babies Coalition, the White House Office of Science and Technology Policy, other agencies—including NICHD, and

SIDS Rate and Back Sleeping (1998–2006)

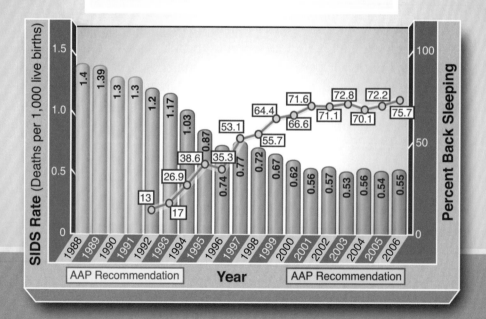

Figure shows that the SIDS rate declined as the percent of back sleeping increased.

other organizations. Safe sleep messages from the Back to Sleep campaign and other healthy pregnancy and healthy infant messages have gone to the program's more than 90,000 subscribers.

Continuing to Refine the Message

In addition, the NICHD and leaders of the Back to Sleep campaign are constantly seeking ways to better understand what factors contribute to the success or failure of safe sleep outreach. For example, the Study of Attitudes and Factors Affecting Infant Care (SAFE) aims to better understand what makes people follow or not follow specific safe sleep messages related to infant sleep position, bed sharing, and pacifier use. SAFE focuses on understanding attitudes and barriers to behavioral change. Findings from this study will help the Back to Sleep campaign and other outreach efforts further refine their messages and their outreach methods to make them more effective and successful.

The NICHD will continue its multifaceted efforts to understand SIDS and eliminate it as a cause of infant death. The Institute will continue to support and conduct cutting-edge science to understand the causes of and contributors to SIDS as a way to move toward detection and possible prevention. At the same time, the NICHD will continue to refine the Back to Sleep campaign, its messages, and its outreach methods to most effectively reach all parents and caregivers with important safe sleep messages.

Parents Are Ignoring the Back to Sleep Campaign

Heather Sokoloff

In the following viewpoint, Heather Sokoloff contends that many parents are not following back to sleep recommendations or other safe-sleep guidelines for their babies. According to Sokoloff, sleep deprivation is the primary reason that parents are using unsafe sleeping practices such as placing their babies to sleep on their tummies or sleeping with their babies. Heather Sokoloff is a Canadian journalist writing for the Toronto daily newspaper the *Globe and Mail.*

Valerie Telio has heard the warnings again and again: The safest way for a new baby to sleep is on the back, in a crib.

But when her third child, born last summer, turned out to be a terrible sleeper, the Montreal mother brought the baby into her bed. And after nursing, she settled her daughter by placing her on her tummy in the bed.

She's not alone in her nighttime desperation.

SOURCE: Heather Sokoloff, "The New Parent's Dirty Little Secret," *Globe and Mail,* April 10, 2009. Copyright © 2009 by Heather Sokoloff. Reproduced by permission.

Debra Mawas let her son Sean sleep in his swing all night; otherwise he woke every 90 minutes.

Arwen Hunter relied on the bouncy chair to get a few hours' rest during her daughter Sophia's first months.

"I had heard it was bad," says Ms. Hunter, who lives in Toronto. "But I didn't care. I was exhausted."

On other issues, they are the kind of mothers who follow public-health advice to the letter. They breastfeed and make organic purees. They seal off electrical sockets in their homes with safety plugs. Ms. Telio even put a safety gate on her own bed.

Sleep Deprivation

But when it comes to getting through the first few months with a new baby, some of the most vigilant mothers admit to ignoring their doctors' advice and doing whatever it takes to get their babies to sleep.

> FAST FACT
>
> According to First Candle and the National Crib Campaign, the percentage of infants who shared a bed with their parents doubled from 5.5 to 12.8 percent from 1993 to 2004.

"You are so horribly sleep-deprived, you would do anything," Ms. Mawas says.

"You can't judge until you've been through it."

A Quebec coroner's report, released [in April 2009], found that a two-month-old baby died [in 2008] of asphyxiation after his mother put him to sleep in a car seat after a restless night. The coroner, Jacques Robinson, explained that the head of a baby sleeping in a car seat can bend far forward, restricting the upper respiratory passages and cutting off oxygen.

Dr. Robinson is recommending that health and social service agencies make new parents aware of these potential risks.

But parents of sleepless newborns say yet another public-health warning is likely to result in more guilt and anxiety.

Ms. Telio, for example, says she would regularly wake "in a cold sweat," convinced she had rolled over on her daughter—a risk associated with co-sleeping.

Some young mothers are so exhausted in the first few months with a new baby that even the most vigilant ones may ignore a doctor's advice. (© Mark McEvoy/Alamy)

Tracey Ruiz, a birthing and postpartum specialist who is known as the "sleep doula," says parents are already under tremendous strain from sleep deprivation.

She has a roster of clients who do everything from driving their babies around in car seats for hours to climbing into the crib with their newborns to get them to sleep.

"The desperation you see in these families is ridiculous."

Ms. Ruiz says her clients often lack community support to get them through the first few difficult months of caring for a newborn.

Many new parents live far away from their families. Many are discharged quickly from the hospital after giving birth and get little assistance during the postpartum period.

As a result, many new mothers do not tell their health-care providers that they are not going completely by the book when it comes to their babies' sleep.

"They aren't honest because they know they are going to get heck for it," Ms. Ruiz says.

When Natalie Morales, an anchorwoman at NBC's *Today* show, recently posted on a parenting website that she put her colicky son to sleep on his tummy, her message was met with cheers from other parents in the same situation. "We can both sleep better at night because of it," Ms. Morales wrote. "Is that such a bad thing?"

Breaking the Rules

Ms. Hunter, who co-slept with her daughter and let her sleep five to six hours in the bouncy chair, says she "rolled her eyes" when she heard the chair may be bad for her daughter's physical development.

"It's hard to remember all the rules that I broke." Ms. Hunter says.

The Canadian Pediatric Society [CPS] attempted to take a "harm-reduction" approach by creating a set of guidelines for safer co-sleeping. The practice is associated with suffocation and sudden infant death syndrome, but can be made more safe if parents remove pillows and duvets, make sure there is no possibility of entrapment between the mattress and wall, and do not take drugs or drink, says Denis Leduc, a Montreal pediatrician who co-authored the CPS position on creating a safe sleep environment for infants.

"If you eliminate all those things and you are breast-feeding, chances are you are going to be okay," Dr. Leduc says.

The problem is also being addressed by several U.S. jurisdictions in which low-income parents are given training in soothing methods outlined in Harvey Karp's bestseller *The Happiest Baby on the Block.* According to Dr. Karp,

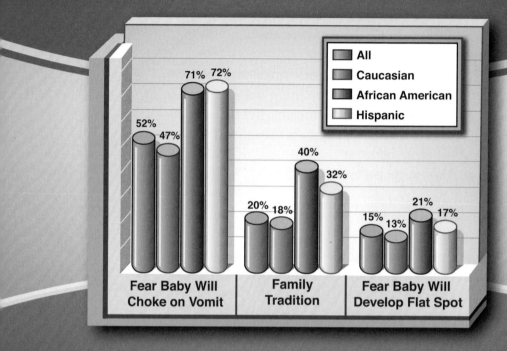

Reasons for Not Placing Baby to Sleep on Back

Legend:
- All
- Caucasian
- African American
- Hispanic

Fear Baby Will Choke on Vomit: 52%, 47%, 71%, 72%

Family Tradition: 20%, 18%, 40%, 32%

Fear Baby Will Develop Flat Spot: 15%, 13%, 21%, 17%

Taken from: Compiled by editor; based on data from Safe Sleep Campaign 2000 SIDS Awareness Survey, US Consumer Products Safety Commission, April 2000.

while back sleeping is the safest position for babies, it is also the least comforting.

Dr. Karp's book and DVD describe how to combine swaddling, swinging, sucking, positioning and shushing sounds to soothe newborns.

He says infant crying and sleeplessness are the top causes of postpartum depression, shaken-baby syndrome and breastfeeding failure.

Vaccines May Cause SIDS

Ingri Cassel

Immunizations are harmful and cause sudden infant death syndrome, asserts Ingri Cassel in the following viewpoint. Cassel tells the tragic story of the sudden death of Idaho infant Vance Walker, just days after he received a series of vaccinations. According to Cassel, Vance's mother, Shelly, blames the vaccines for her son's death and has dedicated herself to informing other parents about the dangers of infant vaccination. Cassel praises Ms. Walker and hopes that all parents will hear her message and forgo their children's vaccinations. Ingri Cassel is the director of Vaccination Liberation, an antivaccination organization.

S helly Walker's heartwrenching story made the front page of the [*Spokane, WA*] *Spokesman-Review* newspaper on December 22, 2007, with the provocative headline, "Did vaccines kill?"

The headline shook up many residents [in northwest Idaho] as they prepared for Christmas with their families.

SOURCE: Ingri Cassel, "Cluster of 'SIDS' Deaths in North Idaho Prompt Parents to Blame Vaccines; Doctors, Government Deny Vaccine Link," *Idaho Observer*, February 22, 2008. Reproduced by permission.

The story highlighted Shelly's shock when she discovered her son Vance in his crib unresponsive and limp. Blood was crusted under his eyes and a bloody foam was coming from his mouth onto the blanket lying beside him. The following is from *The Spokesman-Review* story:

FAST FACT

According to the US Institute of Medicine, one study found that SIDS accounted for 47.6 percent of deaths reported to the Vaccine Adverse Events Reporting System (VAERS) from July 1990 through June 1997.

"My baby was so healthy," said Shelly Walker, 39, of Hayden [Idaho]. "He was extremely full of life, energy and vitality."

In the early morning of Sept. 15, less than three days after Vance Vernon Walker received a round of vaccines at Lakeside Pediatric and Adolescent Medicine in Coeur d'Alene, his mother awoke to a parent's worst nightmare. "It was about 5:15 AM. I woke up and thought, 'He's not making any noise!'" Walker recalled. "I went to pick him up and then I screamed."

Her 16 1/2-pound boy was warm and his lips were still pink, but he wasn't moving. Blood was crusted beneath his eyes and his clothes and toys were covered with a bloody froth. As her husband, Brian, 46, called 911, Walker worked frantically to resuscitate their child. But in the emergency room at Kootenai Medical Center, doctors said Vance had been dead for several hours.

The Proud Parents

Brian and Shelly Walker had waited several years to have their first child. They were proud and doting parents who were absolutely thrilled with each developmental milestone Vance achieved.

Shelly had worked for many years at Pilgrim's, a local health food store. Over the years, many well-meaning customers had exposed her to the vaccine controversy, but it never dawned on her that vaccines could actually be deadly and wouldn't necessarily protect her son from infectious diseases.

The Walkers were planning a trip to Mexico in October so she got a passport for Vance, the youngest child to receive a passport in 2007, according to Shelly. Naturally, the Walkers reasoned, receiving "protective" vaccines would be important while traveling to a country having a lower standard of living than Americans are used to.

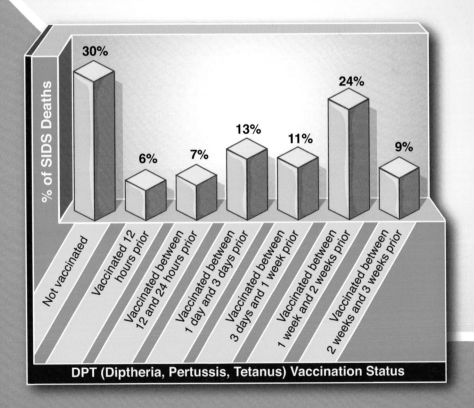

SIDS Deaths and DPT Vaccination

Based on a study of 70 SIDS cases presented by neurologist William Torch at the 34th Annual Meeting of the *American Academy of Neurology*, Washington, D.C., April 25–May 1, 1982.

% of SIDS Deaths

- 30% — Not vaccinated
- 6% — Vaccinated 12 hours prior
- 7% — Vaccinated between 12 and 24 hours prior
- 13% — Vaccinated between 1 day and 3 days prior
- 11% — Vaccinated between 3 days and 1 week prior
- 24% — Vaccinated between 1 week and 2 weeks prior
- 9% — Vaccinated between 2 weeks and 3 weeks prior

DPT (Diptheria, Pertussis, Tetanus) Vaccination Status

Taken from: Compiled by editor; based on data from Harris Coulter and Barbara Loe Fisher, *A Shot in the Dark*, 1991.

A Visit to the "Doctor"

Vance received a shot of Pediarix, a 5-in-1 shot for diphtheria, tetanus, pertussis, hepatitis B and polio; a shot of Prevnar, seven pneumococcal viruses plus diphtheria toxoid; and Rotateq, the new rotavirus vaccine given orally and containing four viruses associated with infant diarrhea. That adds up to 19 different pathogens given to a four-month-old infant in less than 15 minutes when you consider that Pediarix contains three polio strains.

"It Was the Vaccines, Wasn't It?"

When Brian and Shelly were in the emergency room still in a state of shock, Shelly blurted out, "It was the vaccines, wasn't it? Was this from the damn vaccines?"

When her desperate plea for confirmation was met with denial and attempts to comfort her, a seed was planted that has since grown into a force that has become public health's worse nightmare—more and more parents speaking out as a result of their own tragic experience with the devastation caused by vaccines.

The Vaccination Debate

KXLY, a Spokane television station, publicized its airing of "The Vaccination Debate" for a week prior to the February 5, 2008, short, five-minute news broadcast in which Shelly's tragic experience was highlighted.

News reporter Kalae Chock interviewed Shelly, their attorney in Virginia, David Terzian, who filed their case with the national Vaccine Injury Compensation Program and Spokane pediatrician Bob Maixner. The Vaccination Debate was aired on the morning news, evening news and late evening news that day. . . .

Leading up to the showing of this news segment, Kalae Chock, also a new mom, had added Vaccination Debate segments to her ongoing internet blog. . . . For many parents, having this forum provided by our local news station is BIG news.

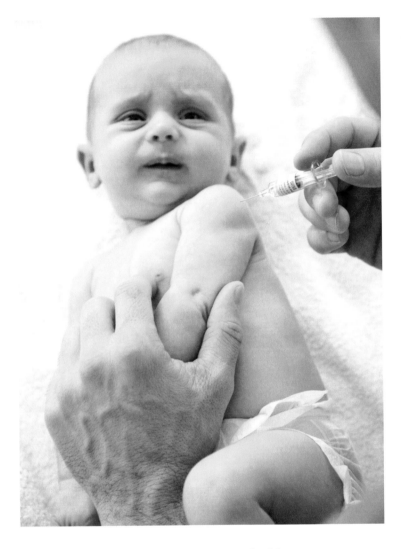

Many parents think that vaccinations played a role in the SIDS death of their child. (Phanie/Photo Researchers, Inc.)

"Karen" stated the following on the blog:

Kalae, you took a very controversial subject and did a wonderful job showing both sides. Giving your children shots is not so cut and dried as we are led to believe. 23 years ago when my child had her first shots, I was a young mom that didn't know very much. I didn't know that my baby was having a seizure. My mom had to tell me that babies don't usually roll their eyes like that and shake. I was so angry and scared that my baby might not be okay. Luckily, she is, but I wish I had known the most important thing: I had a choice. I didn't have to have her go through that. The "authorities" make parents think it is mandatory and the law that your kids have to have shots. I hope that every parent that saw your series will realize that they do have a choice, a personal choice that does not have to be defended to anyone. I wish the slogan would be "Shots: Your child, your choice."

Great job and thank you!

Kalae Chock's ninth blog on the Vaccination Debate states that the original purpose for the Vaccination Debate report was "to share Shelly Walker's story and to explain the government's compensation program for vaccine related deaths and injuries."

It is clear from her comments that she had no idea how controversial the vaccine topic had become.

In the meantime, Shelly Walker is one mom on a mission—sharing her story as a means of alerting other moms to the real dangers inherent in all vaccines. She has made several copies of an article by Dr. Tedd Koren, "Crib Death or Vaccine Death?" in which he cites that SIDS is the second most common cause of infant death with 10,000 deaths annually. . . .

Shelly writes, "I hope and pray that this tragedy never occurs in your family. With the knowledge I have acquired since his death I can firmly say that I will never vaccinate a child under the age of 24 months again, if at all. I lacked knowledge to make the best choice. I hope this empowers you to combat the darkness and seek the knowledge necessary to make the best decision."

We second Shelly's sentiments and pray that people will "investigate before they vaccinate" since the only "informed" choice is complete avoidance and refusal. We are extremely grateful for Shelly Walker for taking the tragic loss of her only child and sharing what she has learned with others, passionately and publicly.

Vaccines Are Not a Risk Factor for SIDS

US Centers for Disease Control and Prevention

The US Centers for Disease Control and Prevention (CDC) is a federal government agency that monitors diseases and provides health information to the public. In the following viewpoint, the CDC says that despite the fact that the age at which babies begin their first series of vaccinations corresponds to the peak age for sudden infant death syndrome (SIDS), infant vaccinations are safe and do not cause SIDS. According to the CDC, several studies have been performed, and none of them could find a link between vaccinations and SIDS. According to the CDC, most SIDS deaths are due to babies sleeping on their stomachs and other factors.

From 2 to 4 months old, babies begin their primary course of vaccinations. This is also the peak age for sudden infant death syndrome (SIDS). The timing of these two events has led some people to believe they might be related. However, studies have concluded that vaccinations are not a risk factor for SIDS.

SOURCE: "Sudden Infant Death Syndrome (SIDS) and Vaccines," US Centers for Disease Control and Prevention, January 15, 2010.

Studies Show Vaccines Are Safe

With babies receiving multiple doses of vaccines during their first year of life and SIDS being the leading cause of death in babies between one month and one year of age, CDC [Centers for Disease Control and Prevention] has led research studies to look for possible linkages. Results from studies below and continued monitoring reassure us about the safety of vaccines.

The Institute of Medicine (IOM) released a report [titled] *Immunization Safety Review: Vaccination and Sudden Unexpected Death in Infancy* in 2003. The committee reviewed epidemiologic evidence focusing on SIDS, all sudden unexpected death in infancy, and neonatal death (infant death, whether sudden or not, during the first 4 weeks of life). The committee also looked for possible relationships between SIDS and the individual vaccines diphtheria-tetanus-whole-cell pertussis (DTwP), DTaP, HepB [Hepatitis B], Hib [*Haemophiles influenzae* type B which causes bacterial meningitis], and polio; and specific combinations of vaccines. The committee did not find enough evidence to show vaccines cause SIDS.

A study using Vaccine Safety Datalink (VSD) data, which included children who were covered by a managed care organization health plan, found no association between immunization and deaths in young children. The study investigated deaths in children one month to 7 years of age between 1991 and 1995. Data were analyzed by comparing vaccination histories for each vaccine during the week and month prior to the date of death for each child. Five hundred and seventeen deaths occurred between 1991 and 1995, most (59%) during the first year of life. Of these deaths, the results did not show an association between immunizations and childhood deaths.

> **FAST FACT**
>
> The World Health Organization (WHO) estimates that 2 million child deaths were prevented by vaccinations in 2003.

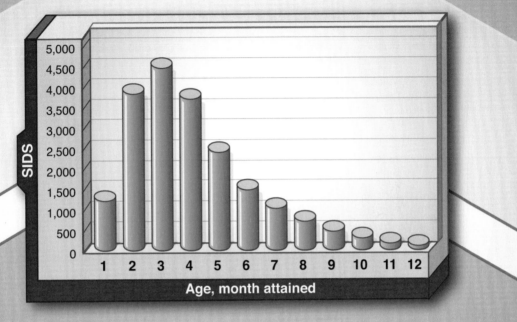

Age Distribution of SIDS

SIDS

Age, month attained

Note: Based on approximately 20,000 SIDS Deaths.

Taken from: David T. Mage and Maria Donner, "A Unifying Theory for SIDS," *International Journal of Pediatrics*, 2009.

Studies looked at the age distribution and seasonality of deaths reported to the Vaccine Adverse Event Reporting System (VAERS). SIDS and VAERS reports following DTP vaccination, and SIDS and VAERS reports following hepatitis B vaccination found no association between SIDS and vaccination.

VAERS also monitors the safety of vaccines. Through VAERS the U.S. Food and Drug Administration carefully investigates all deaths following vaccination that are reported to VAERS.

As a result of the American Academy of Pediatrics' 1992 recommendation to place healthy babies on their backs to sleep, and the success of the National Institute of Child Health and Human Development's Back to Sleep

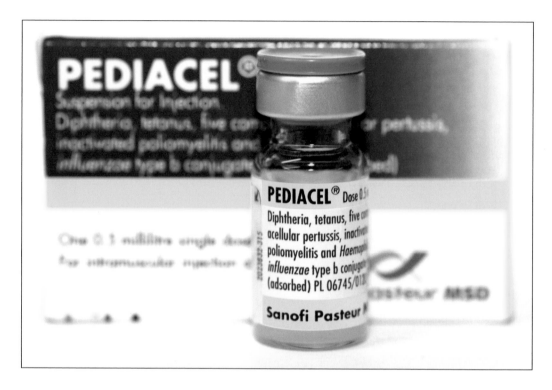

The Institute of Medicine tested various baby vaccines, like the whooping cough vaccine Pediacel, and did not find enough evidence to link vaccines to SIDS. (Dr. P. Marazzi/ Photo Researchers, Inc.)

campaign, fewer SIDS deaths are reported. According to "Targeting SIDS: A Strategic Plan":

- Between 1992 and 1998, the proportion of infants placed to sleep on their stomachs declined from about 70 percent to about 17 percent.
- Between 1992 and 1998, the SIDS rate declined by about 40 percent, from 1.2 per 1,000 live births to 0.72 per 1,000 live births.

These results tell us that most SIDS deaths are due to factors like sleeping on their stomachs, cigarette smoke exposure, and mild respiratory infections.

CHAPTER 3

Personal Experiences with SIDS

We Were Young Then and Did Not Know About SIDS

Jonathan and Bridgette Alexander

In the following viewpoint, Bridgette and Jonathan Alexander describe the sudden death of their infant son Julian. According to the Alexanders, they did not know about the Back to Sleep campaign or that African Americans face a higher risk of sudden infant death syndrome (SIDS) than whites or Hispanics. Since the heartbreaking loss of Julian, the Alexanders have dedicated their lives to educating themselves about SIDS, informing other African American families about the disorder, and finding a cure for SIDS. The Alexander family resides in Texas.

W e were blessed with a happy, bouncy, baby boy we named Julian Jamaal Alexander [on December 7, 2004]. We first noticed his cry, his soft eyes, the way he smelled, and his beautiful hair. Julian loved to eat and loved to sleep. We nicknamed him fat-fat since he got so big so fast. He had a smile that would light up a room and a coo that just melted

Photo on previous page. When a young mother experiences the SIDS-related death of a child, she often questions how it could have happened. (© Angela Farley/ Shutterstock.com)

SOURCE: Bridgette Alexander and Jonathan Alexander, "Julian's Story, How SIDS Took His Life and Changed Ours on December 6, 2004," simonproject.org, 2006. Reproduced by permission of the author.

your heart. He was a joy to see after a hard day, his giggle made everything okay. He motivated us to be better and do more.

A Morning That Changed Our Lives Forever

The morning of March 24, 2005, changed our lives forever. We woke at 7:33 AM to find our precious baby lying in bed and what we thought was sleeping. We went to move Julian to find he wasn't breathing. We performed C.P.R. [cardiopulmonary resuscitation], as we were both certified and called 911. The ambulance came and paramedics took our baby. We rushed to the local hospital and upon our arrival a nurse sat us down. She said, "I'm sorry, but he is gone"; our hearts cracked, tears fell, and emotions went wild. We were taken to a cold, dark room and saw our baby's lifeless little body lying there. We took him together in our arms and held him and cried. We were so confused and didn't know what happened, how, and most of all why. Anger set in and so did guiltiness, we blamed ourselves, we questioned God, and we pointed fingers.

Julian was buried March 29, 2005. His service was beautiful; fit for a little prince. We never noticed how many lives he touched until that day. There were so many people: family, extended family, friends, colleagues, and many others who just wanted to say a last goodbye. We talked about it everyday after his death; in the back of our minds it was always there, but when we received his autopsy report we were speechless. It read: cause of death—sudden infant death syndrome. We became S.I.D.S parents, and our angel was a victim of S.I.D.S.

> **FAST FACT**
>
> According to the US Centers for Disease Control and Prevention, in 2006 the death rate from SIDS for African Americans was 103.8 deaths per 100,000 live births, compared with 55.6 deaths per 100,000 live births for non-Hispanic whites.

We Did Not Think It Could Happen to Us

We were aware of S.I.D.S from close friends of ours who lost their child years before. But like many we were naive, we thought, "This couldn't happen to us." We slept with our first child next to us and he survived so there was no doubt in our minds; we assumed Julian would be fine. We were uneducated then to this monster called S.I.D.S, so we started attending meetings and reading more on it. We took action to learn and educate others. We wanted to know what took our baby. We wanted to help others protect their babies. We express our emotions to all that will hear.

In the 1990's the "safe sleep" campaign was going on. We were young then, children ourselves, and didn't know what that was about. Now as adults and parents ourselves we want to reach out to our peers. Many young parents don't know about or even remember the "safe sleep" campaign. We want to get the word out to our generation about S.I.D.S, the correct "room sharing" guidelines, and how they can protect their children.

As young, African American parents, we want to educate other African American families on the rise of S.I.D.S in our ethnic group. Julian will forever live on for we have dedicated ourselves to telling his story, learning more about S.I.D.S, educating others, and succeeding in finding a cause to sudden infant death syndrome.

A SIDS Story of Joy, Heartbreak, and Healing

Stephanie Williams

In the following story, Stephanie Williams tells about the loss of her ten-month-old son Jacob to sudden infant death syndrome (SIDS). Stephanie writes about Jacob's "wonderful hugs and slobbery kisses" and the joys of being his mother. She talks about the day SIDS took him away, and how it began like any other day, but how it ended with unbearable heartbreak. Then she describes how she and her husband coped with life after SIDS by clinging to each other and to their religious faith. Finally, she talks about healing and being a parent again but never forgetting little Jacob. Stephanie Williams is the president of Tiny Handprints, an organization dedicated to helping other families who have suffered a SIDS loss.

After a five-year relationship and one year of marriage, my husband and I decided we were "ready" for children. On August 1, 2005, we discovered we were pregnant with our first child. Ladd was convinced from the moment he saw the positive pregnancy test that

SOURCE: Stephanie Williams, "Jacob's Story," tinyhandprints.org, 2010. Reproduced by permission of the author.

we were having a boy, and he was right. My pregnancy was uneventful with the exception of a "gestational diabetic" diagnosis at 26 weeks. My case was mild, so it meant only diet and blood sugar monitoring from home. That's what I get for eating bags of peanut M&M's early in my pregnancy, using the excuse "it's what the baby wants!"

Jacob Hughes Williams Arrives

On March 14, 2006, I started having contractions. Since I was past the 36 week mark (36 weeks and 2 days gestation), my OB [obstetrician] let my labor continue. Ten hours later, Jacob Hughes Williams was born, weighing 5 lbs, 14 ounces. Although a little early, he was perfectly healthy! We joked that he was just excited to get out and see the world. Little did we know, we would come to appreciate those extra few weeks we shared, as he would fulfill his purpose on this earth and return home to be with the Lord in less time than we had anticipated.

Besides a short stay in Vanderbilt Medical Center for jaundice, Jacob never had any health problems. Right from the start, he was a very happy baby, always smiling, and content with almost anything. He met all the usual baby milestones of rolling over, crawling, and standing by himself. He could say "mama" and was working on saying "dada." He was exceptionally healthy, and he gave the most wonderful hugs and slobbery kisses. He was his daddy's pride and joy and was a real "mama's boy" at heart. He stayed at home with Mommy three days a week, and spent the other two days playing with his buddies, Gavin, 7 and Katelyn, 2, at Laura's house, his babysitter. Jacob was perfect, and our world was right.

On January 23, 2007, we woke up and ate breakfast. Jacob watched his favorite show, *Higglytown Heroes,* while I got ready for work. I dropped Jacob off at Laura's house around 8:00 that morning. He would spend the day there, and I would pick him up at 5 PM. He spent the morning playing, just like every other day. Laura laid Jacob down for his nap around 1:30 that afternoon. She checked on him a little while later to find him resting comfortably in his crib. She went to check on him again . . . only this time he looked different, eerily still. She touched his leg—it was cold. She picked him up and ran to the phone, dialed 911 and attempted to perform CPR [cardiopulmonary resuscitation] while she waited for the paramedics to arrive.

It was 4:00 and I was ready to go home, to go see my sweet baby. I started to get excited every day around that time, anxious to see his smiling face as he crawled to greet me at the door. I was in my coworker's office when I heard my cell phone ring. I was busy, so I let my voicemail pick it up. It rang again. . . . "It must be my mother" I thought. "She'll leave a message and I'll call her back when I leave." My office direct line started to ring, then my cell phone again. This time, I answered it. It was my husband, Ladd. "Where have you been, I've been calling you!" I was not prepared for the words that followed. . . . "Something's wrong with Jacob. You need to get to Laura's house NOW!"

The Whole World Stopped Turning

It felt as if suddenly the whole world stopped turning. My boss, Liz and one of my co-workers were walking by my office as I said "Oh God No!" They rushed into my office and asked what was wrong. As I stood there holding the phone in my hand, I managed to mutter the words I had just heard, "Something's wrong with Jacob." "What's wrong?" they asked. "I don't know." "What do we need to do, Steph?" Again came the words, "I don't know." "Are they taking him to the hospital?" "I don't know" was all I could say. As I stood there paralyzed, my mind racing, Liz took the phone from me and dialed Laura's number. A man answered: "This is sergeant such-and-such with the Nolensville police department." "Can I speak to Laura?" Liz asked. "Ma'am we have a situation here and she can't come to the phone right now," he replied. "My name is Liz and I'm here with Jacob's mother. Can you tell me what's going on?" He told her the ambulance was on its way to a local hospital, and then he hung up the phone. . . .

Life After SIDS

The next morning, I rolled over and looked at the clock. It was six thirty in the morning, the time I'd usually hear Jacob cooing and hollering at me from his crib. I'd walk in to find him standing up holding onto the rail, smiling at me and excited to start his day—every day. The horrifying images from the previous evening returned to me like a tidal wave crashing down over my body. I began to sob "I can't do this, Ladd. I don't think I'm going to make it through this!" I was his mother, what was he suppose to do without me? What was I suppose to do without him?

Looking back, the days that followed are all a blur. I remember making funeral arrangements and bits and pieces from the services. There were over 350 people who signed the guest book at the funeral, including members of the Nolensville Rescue Squad, Police and Fire departments. Every hug I received made me cry, and every time I cried, the incredible load I carried began to feel a little lighter. Over the next several weeks our mailbox overflowed with cards and letters—literally, at least 20 each day for the first three weeks—from friends and family, and even more from people we had never met, but who had heard of us through friends and wanted to let us know they were praying for us. I remember thinking we must have had half the world praying for us, and we could feel it.

Clinging to Jesus and Each Other

So what did we do that helped us through it? There were a number of things. The most important one was to cling to Jesus. We knew He was the only one who could provide the grace and comfort we so desperately needed. Only He could restore the joy in our lives that once was Jacob, and only He could assure us that we would all be together again someday. We leaned on Him, and he carried us through it. Number two—cling to each other. No one knew the depth of our pain like the other, so we leaned on each other. Ladd and I each had our own unique ways of dealing with our grief, but tried to be patient with each other, and did the best we could to understand the other's process. Other helpful things included gathering as much information as we could about SIDS/SUID [sudden infant death syndrome/sudden unexpected infant death] to help us answer all the questions we had, reading grief books, seeing a grief counselor, taking a vacation, and connecting with other grieving families.

How do you even begin to put back together the pieces of your life when the most important part is missing? One breath at a time, then one day at a time; by lying flat on your face in the palm of God's hand until you have the strength to lift your head to look to him. It reminds me of a child learning to walk. . . . It starts by lifting the head, then pushing up with your hands until you've gained enough strength to push up onto your knees. Eventually you're able to stand, and then life begins to move forward again. Slowly, yes, but it does move forward.

We learned early on not to measure our process against others, but to take one day at a time, allowing as much time as was necessary for us to take on the projects of selecting a headstone, cleaning up his room, etc. About two weeks after we buried Jacob, we disassembled his crib, but only because the agony of seeing it empty was more than that of taking it down. A few weeks later, we began to pack up his room. Someone had given us a small wooden trunk to store his keepsakes in that was engraved with his name and dates. In it, we put all his special things: a lock of his hair, his favorite toys, his baby book and a pair of

FAST FACT

According to the American Academy of Pediatrics, of the approximately 20 percent of SIDS deaths that occur while a child is at day care, one-third occur in the first week, and one-half of these occur on the first day.

his favorite pajamas (he was so snuggly in his pajamas!). Then I sat down with a notepad and listed everything I knew about him, everything I wanted to make sure I never forgot. It came together so well that I added pictures and actually had it bound into a book, printed copies, and distributed it to family members. We kept three copies for ourselves—one for us, and two for other children we hoped to be blessed with later.

New Bundles of Joy

Then, in early March, a little less than five weeks after we buried our first child, we found out we were pregnant with another. In May, we met a couple who had just lost their six-month-old baby girl, Landrie Grace. We encouraged one another and grieved collectively, seemingly bonded together by the similar turns our lives had taken. They could see in us what lay ahead, and we could see in them how far we had come. Five weeks after they lost Landrie, they asked us to dinner to tell us that they too were expecting another child. In June, we found out ours was a girl and in September, they discovered they were having a boy.

On November 14, 2007, Abigail Grace Williams was born. On January 23, 2008, exactly one year after we lost Jacob, Owen was born [to the other couple]. It has been a roller coaster ride for sure. But as time passes, the ups are much more frequent than the downs. The bitter memories of that day are fading, giving way to more bittersweet memories of Jacob's life. Not a day goes by that we don't think about Jacob, that we don't miss him, that we don't long to hold him again. But as a shattered vase is put back together, once piece at a time, so our lives are being restored. Our "new normal" is one of overwhelming joy, peace and love.

Without a doubt, Abby's birth and life have been crucial in our journey. Did she replace Jacob—absolutely not. But she did fill that emptiness in our arms that his loss left us with. She's definitely her own person: strong-willed and stubborn like her daddy, and sweet, loving, and exceptionally smart. We've been a little over-protective, but who wouldn't be? She knows no difference, only lots of love and affection from everyone around her.

Update: We found out in May 2009 that we were expecting another bundle of joy! Currin Ladd Williams was born in late December, 2009. We're excited to see what our newest addition will bring to our lives!

One day, when we're ready, and when Abby and Currin are old enough to understand, we'll tell them all about their big brother Jacob.

A Father's Story About Losing His Son to SIDS

Marvin Job

In the following viewpoint, Marvin Job provides a father's perspective on losing a child to sudden infant death syndrome (SIDS). Marvin remembers the day his infant son Spenser died in 1987. This was before the national Back to Sleep campaign. The family was camping, and Spenser was crabby from a cold. Marvin had laid him down to sleep on his stomach on a sleeping bag in the tent. Now Marvin is wracked with pain and guilt over Spenser's death. Marvin is only able to cope and go on after Spenser's death because of his faith in God and his belief in Jesus. Marvin Job posted his story to the website Thoughts About God, which provides articles and stories to help people grow in their relationship with God.

Our son Spenser died of SIDS (Sudden Infant Death Syndrome) on August 22, 1987, when he was almost five months of age.

Zac, my 1½ year old son and myself were busy getting our new home in shape for the arrival of Spenser Tyrone

SOURCE: Marvin Job, "My Son Died of SIDS," thoughts-about-god. com, 2010. Used with permission of Thoughts About God website, www.thoughts-about-god.com.

Job. We had just moved into our house a couple days before. We still needed railings on the stairs, tile in the front entrance and a lot of boxes unpacked.

Spenser Tyrone Job Arrives!

Val gave birth to Spenser on March 27, 1987. As much as your children change your lives from their birth onwards, I never expected the changes that lay ahead for Val and myself.

Spenser was one of those kids that could eat a great meal (bottle) and then throw up half of it on you when you weren't looking. I remember one time heading into town with Zac and Spenser (three months old) and seeing the two boys holding hands and just talking to each other. To me it looked like they were planning their first 2-on-2 basketball team.

Four and a half months went by very quiet. It was now mid August. Val just left with Spenser to help cook at Camp Tulahead. For one week Zac and I were on our own. I didn't realize then that in six days my life would take a change in a direction that would affect me for the rest of my life.

I remember Sunday morning looking out of our upstairs living room window seeing the neighbor kids and their parents play by the swings at the park down the street. They were laughing and having fun. A car drove up to the mailbox across the street, the lady picked up her mail and left, just like many others did. People were walking on the sidewalk, cars were going up and down our street. Everyone's life was moving at its normal pace. No one seemed to care that my world had come to a complete stop, that even though I may have looked normal on the outside I was in so much pain on the inside that I felt as if there was a hole blasted through my chest—only it wasn't a clean hole. The edges of the hole felt as though they were torn all around and the entire way through. I didn't know that you could feel so much physical pain from an emotional loss.

Finding Spenser

The day before, Saturday, August 22, 1987, Spenser died. I was young and didn't expect life to throw me a curve like that. We were camping at the group campsite at Allouette Provincial Park with our young couples group from church. Val met Zac and me there on the second day of the weekend as she came straight from Camp Tulahead. Spenser had a minor cold that week and was a bit crabby, probably from the long drive. I remember putting Spenser to bed on his stomach, in the tent, on top of one of our sleeping bags. Twenty minutes later I went back to check on him. He was in a different position, very quiet and face down into the sleeping bag. As I rotated his head to help him breathe better while sleeping, I saw blue colouring around his mouth and under his nose. As I shook him to wake him, major panic struck my body. He wasn't waking up. The next thing I can remember was running out of the tent carrying a limp Spenser yelling, "He is dead." From then on until the ambulance came is a fog to me. All I remember is that a friend of mine did CPR [cardiopulmonary resuscitation] on Spenser until the paramedics took over.

> **FAST FACT**
>
> According to the National Infant Sleep Position Survey, in 1992 70.1 percent of parents placed their babies to sleep on the babies' stomachs.

The next few hours were very draining on Val and myself. We spent those long hours praying, not even knowing what to pray for ([for Spenser] to live or to die, as [he] had been without oxygen for quite some time) and we spent time crying. As I think back, I don't even remember where Zac was, except that he was with one of our friends.

What Now, God?

Zac was two years old then. Even though we tried to tell him his brother was now with Jesus in heaven I don't really think it made real sense to him. That next day I saw Zac sitting on the property peg in the back corner of our lot, so I went out to see what he was doing. He told me that he was making a phone call to God to see how Spenser was doing. It wasn't till a month later that Zac would cry wondering when Spenser would come back.

That next day on Sunday, August 23, I remember a lot of people coming and going and I remember, as I said already, looking out of our living room window. The rest of the things I remember happened on the inside. Have you ever wondered what to think? What to feel? What was happening? Life did not prepare me for the death of my son. The emotions that I had were all mixed up and included the normal emotions of loss and heartache but with an added sense of non-reality. At times I expected Spenser to start crying for food, the next minute I was trying to make a deal with God to trade places with Spenser.

Was It My Fault?

I had feelings of guilt for what had happened. I really didn't want to deal with Spenser on Saturday because he was grumpy and crying. What kind of Dad would not want to spend time with his son after not seeing him for the past week? For the longest time I felt I killed my own son—that I put him on sleeping material that was too soft that he could suffocate on. Even after the autopsy came back, death by Sudden Infant Death Syndrome, I questioned for a long time and still to this day wonder if I wasn't so disinterested in dealing with a crying child, would I have paid attention more to how I put him to bed. Would Spenser be alive today? Did I kill my own son?

Isolation began to set in quickly. None of my friends could relate to what Val and I were going through. Our thinking changed. Many things became trivial. Our reason for having another child, as hard as it seemed to us at the time, was to have more than one just in case another one dies. When I would look at someone's baby I wouldn't look to see it smile, I would look at the chest or back to see if he or she was breathing. Some of my friends didn't know what to say to me, so they didn't say anything. Two years later one of my friends came up to me in tears, finally able to talk to me normally as we did before.

Over the next few months and years, although less frequent with time, my emotions, which I never had before, were uncontrollable at the most inconvenient of times. I was told that time heals. Well, I discovered that in time you also forget. It was good that in time I forgot the pain of Spenser's death, but it was forgetting his voice, his touch and his character—I would feel guilty that I was forgetting my own son. I felt ripped off that my friends got to have all their kids grow up with them, and what memories I had were fading. To this day I only have a few real strong memories of Spenser and find myself guarding them.

"I Will Never Leave You"

Hebrews 4:12 tells us that God is always with us, He will not leave us. I learned this as a young boy. I started to grasp for something that was constant in my life, something that would not change, someone that was there yesterday and would be there tomorrow—God. God became a stronghold in my life. On that Sunday morning of August 23, 1987 as I looked out the window of my living room at the normality of life in the presence of my chaos, I remember feeling glad that someday I will see my son again. I also felt sad that some of the people in the park across the street playing with their kids more than likely do not have that same assurance of salvation that will make reunion in heaven possible.

During this time my relationship with Val became a more important part of my life. We heard that child deaths cause many marriages to break up. I could not understand how that could be, as I wanted Val close to me more than ever. We went through our grieving together. We needed each other.

Jesus Gave His Life for Us

One thing I have come to understand a little better through my time of grief and years of contemplating the short life and death of Spenser, is that I would not want to give one of my children's lives up for others—to the point of death so that others could live. God did just that. In the verse John 3:16 we recognize that God the Father gave us His only son Jesus to die on the cross, but do we realize what God the Father must have gone through seeing his son hang on the cross. If I had the power to save my son I would have. God had the power to save his son and yet He chose not to. God loves me so much that He chose to allow His son to die for me.

I know in my own heart that God had a purpose for Spenser's life. I trust that one day, when I meet Jesus face to face, I will know and understand completely God's plan for his life.

GLOSSARY

apnea   A period of time when breathing stops or is markedly reduced; apnea commonly occurs during sleep.

autonomic nervous system (ANS)   A part of the peripheral nervous system that controls organ functions. The ANS controls heart rate, digestion, respiration rate, salivation, perspiration, and many bodily functions that occur below the level of consciousness.

autopsy   A postmortem examination to determine the cause of death.

brain stem   The lower extension of the brain where it connects to the spinal cord. The brain stem plays a vital role in basic attention, arousal, and consciousness.

carbon dioxide (CO_2)   A colorless, odorless gas that is the by-product of cellular metabolism and that is carried by the hemoglobin in the red blood cells and removed from the body via the lungs in exhaled air.

cardiac   Having to do with the heart.

cardiopulmonary   Having to do with both the heart and lungs.

cardiopulmonary resuscitation (CPR)   The emergency substitution of heart and lung action to restore life to someone who has stopped breathing and has no pulse. The two main components of conventional CPR are chest compression to make the heart pump and mouth-to-mouth ventilation to breathe for the victim.

congenital   Existing or present at the time of birth.

cot death   Another name for SIDS, commonly used in the United Kingdom, Ireland, Australia, India, South Africa, and New Zealand.

crib death   Another name for SIDS, commonly used in the United States.

diagnosis of exclusion	A medical diagnosis provided by a process of elimination of other reasonable possibilities.
forensic autopsy	A postmortem examination of a body done in light of legal questions about the cause of death.
gastroesophageal	Pertaining to both the stomach and the esophagus.
gastroesophageal reflux	The backward flow of stomach contents into the esophagus, which frequently causes heartburn because of irritation of the esophagus by stomach acid. Gastroesophageal reflux disease is often referred to by its abbreviation: GERD.
hypoxia	A deficiency of oxygen in the tissues of the body.
infant	Typically used to refer to children between the ages of one month and twelve months. The term *infant* is derived from the Latin word *infans*, meaning "unable to speak" or "speechless."
laryngeal	Having to do with the larynx, or voice box.
larynx	Also called the voice box, it is a two-inch-long, tube-shaped organ located in the throat between the pharynx and the trachea. The larynx contains the vocal cords and produces vocal sound.
obstruction	Blockage of a passageway.
overlaying	A term of ancient usage that refers to the act of smothering a child to death by lying on top of him or her during sleep.
pacifier	An artificial nipple, usually made of plastic, given to soothe infants. A pacifier is called by many colloquial names, including a "binky," a "dummy," a "nuk," and a "soother."
pharynx	A hollow tube about five inches long that starts behind the nose and ends at the top of the trachea (windpipe) and esophagus.
prematurity	An early birth defined by the World Health Organization as a baby born before thirty-seven weeks of gestation.
prone	Lying on the stomach with the face downward.

reflex	A reaction that is involuntary, such as blinking or sneezing.
serotonin	A type of neurotransmitter; i.e., a chemical that transmits messages between nerve cells. Serotonin helps regulate some of the body's involuntary actions, such as breathing, heart rate, and blood pressure during sleep.
sleep apnea	A sleep disorder characterized by abnormal pauses in breathing or instances of abnormally shallow breathing.
sudden unexplained death in childhood (SUDC)	The sudden and unexpected death of a child over the age of twelve months, which remains unexplained after a thorough case investigation is conducted.
sudden unexpected infant death (SUID)	An infant who dies suddenly of no immediately obvious cause; another term for SIDS.
supine	Lying on the back with the face upward.
syndrome	A set of signs and symptoms that tend to occur together and that reflect the presence of a particular disease or an increased chance of developing a particular disease.
tryptophan hydroxylase	An enzyme that helps make serotonin.

CHRONOLOGY

B.C. ca. 1500 to 1300

In ancient Egypt, a mother who was judged to be responsible for overlaying (smothering a child by rolling over him or her in sleep) was sentenced to hold the dead infant for three days and nights.

ca. 1050 to 900

In the Old Testament Book of First Kings, Solomon was brought a woman who was said to have "overlaid" her child: "This woman's child died in the night because she overlaid it." (1 Kings 3:19).

A.D. 100 to 200

In his book *On Midwifery and the Diseases of Women*, Greek pediatrician Soranus of Ephesus instructs mothers and wet nurses (female servants who were nursing or breast-feeding their own child and who also would nurse the baby of their mistress or employer) never to sleep with infants in case they should accidentally fall asleep on the baby and somehow suffocate it.

1834

Dr. S.W. Fearn notes in a letter to the medical journal the *Lancet* his postmortem findings of two children who died suddenly in their sleep without an apparent cause.

1842

Dr. C.A. Lee publishes an article in the *American Journal of Medical Science* on the abnormally large thymus gland in infants as a possible cause of sudden infant death.

1892

Dr. C. Templeman publishes an article in the *Edinburgh Medical Journal* based on his autopsy and investigative findings attributing sudden infant deaths to suffocation. He describes typical pathological findings similar to sudden infant death syndrome.

1945   Dr. P.V. Woolley Jr. publishes an article in the *Journal of Pediatrics* exploring the relationship of mechanical suffocation during infancy to the problem of sudden infant death. He argues that much evidence for the belief that healthy infants die from suffocation rests on folklore.

1953   Drs. J.J. Werne and I. Garrow of the Office of the Medical Examiner in New York City publish the first systematic, documented, detailed, and objective analysis of a series of SIDS autopsies in the *American Journal of Pathology*.

1960s   The Guild for Infant Survival and the National SIDS Foundation, volunteer parent-support organizations, are founded.

1963   First international conference on causes of sudden infant death is held in Seattle, Washington.

1969   Second international conference on causes of sudden death in infants is held in Seattle, Washington. At the conference, the term *SIDS* is coined and defined as the sudden death of any infant or young child that is unexpected by history and for which a thorough postmortem examination fails to demonstrate an adequate cause of death.

1974   The Sudden Infant Death Syndrome Act of 1974 is passed by the US Congress. The law assigns responsibility to the National Institute of Child Health and Human Development (NICHD) to conduct SIDS research.

1979   The World Health Organization recognizes SIDS as an official cause of death.

1989   An expert panel convened by NICHD revises the definition of SIDS to be the sudden death of an infant less than one year of age that remains unexplained after a thorough case investigation, including performance of a complete autopsy, examination of the death scene, and review of the clinical history.

1992   The American Academy of Pediatrics (AAP) issues the recommendation that babies sleep on their backs or sides to reduce the risk of SIDS.

1994   NICHD, along with the AAP and the SIDS Alliance (now First Candle), launches the Back to Sleep campaign, recommending that babies be placed to sleep on their backs.

1996   Publication of Guidelines for Investigation of Sudden Unexplained Infant Deaths by the Centers for Disease Control and Prevention.

1997   The AAP revises its recommendation regarding infant sleep positions, stating that on the back is the preferred position.

1998   The Consumer Product Safety Commission convenes a meeting on the hazards of soft bedding for infant sleep.

2005   The AAP recommends that parents consider offering their baby a pacifier at nap time and bedtime as a way to reduce the risk of SIDS.

ORGANIZATIONS TO CONTACT

The editors have compiled the following list of organizations concerned with the issues debated in this book. The descriptions are derived from materials provided by the organizations. All have publications or information available for interested readers. The list was compiled on the date of publication of the present volume; the information provided here may change. Be aware that many organizations take several weeks or longer to respond to inquiries, so allow as much time as possible.

American Academy of Pediatrics (AAP)
141 Northwest Point Blvd., Elk Grove Village, IL 60007-1098
(847) 434-4000
fax: (847) 434-8000
e-mail: kidsdocs@aap.org
website: www.aap.org

The AAP is an organization of pediatricians committed to the attainment of optimal physical, mental, and social health and well-being for all infants, children, adolescents, and young adults. The AAP issues recommendations and guidelines for infant and child health. AAP publications include *Pediatrics, AAP News, AAP Grand Rounds, NeoReviews*, and *Pediatrics in Review*.

American SIDS Institute
528 Raven Way, Naples, FL 34110
(239) 431-5425
fax: (239) 431-5536
e-mail: prevent@sids.org
website: www.sids.org

The American SIDS Institute is a national nonprofit health-care organization dedicated to the prevention of sudden infant death and the promotion of infant health. The institute funds research about both the cause of sudden infant death and methods of prevention, provides information to the public and medical community, and gives support to families grieving over a SIDS death. The institute's website provides a memorial page for children who have been lost to SIDS.

**CJ Foundation
for SIDS**
HUMC: WFAN
Pediatric Center,
30 Prospect Ave.,
Hackensack, NJ 07601
(201) 996-5301; toll-
free: (888) 8CJ-SIDS
fax: (201) 996-5326
e-mail: info@cjsids.org
website: www.cjsids.org

The mission of the CJ Foundation for SIDS, a national non-profit health organization, is to reduce the risk of future infant deaths, support families who have suffered a loss, and fund medical research so that no more families have to endure the pain of losing an infant. The foundation carries out its mission by providing funding for SIDS research projects, organizations, support programs, and public education and awareness campaigns throughout the nation. The CJ Foundation sponsors conferences and provides myriad posters and pamphlets to educate the public about SIDS. A sister program, the Sudden Unexplained Death in Childhood Program (at www. sudc. org), was created by the CJ Foundation to provide information, support, advocacy, and research services to families affected by a sudden unexpected death in childhood, the cause of which is left undetermined, unclear, or unexplained.

**Eunice Kennedy
Shriver National
Institute of Child
Health and Human
Development
(NICHD)**
NICHD Information
Resource Center
31 Center Dr.,
Bldg. 31, Rm. 2A32,
Bethesda, MD 20892-
2425
(800) 505-CRIB (2742)
fax: (866) 760-5947
e-mail: nichdinforma
tionresourcecenter@
mail.nih.gov
website: www.nichd
.nih.gov/sids

The Eunice Kennedy Shriver National Institute of Child Health and Human Development is one of twenty-nine institutes and centers that make up the National Institutes of Health, the nation's medical research agency. The institute conducts and supports research on all stages of human development, from preconception to adulthood, to better understand the health of children, adults, families, and communities. The NICHD is a primary sponsor of the Back to Sleep campaign and provides education and public outreach on safe-sleep practices for babies. The NICHD publishes a wide variety of reports, pamphlets, fact sheets, and other materials on safe sleeping and many other child-health topics.

First Candle
1314 Bedford Ave.,
Ste. 210, Baltimore,
MD 21208
(800) 221-7437
e-mail: info@first
candle.org
website: www.first
candle.org

Formerly known as the SIDS Alliance, First Candle is a national nonprofit health organization uniting parents, caregivers, and researchers nationwide with government, business, and community service groups to advance infant health and survival. A founding sponsor of the nationwide Back to Sleep campaign, First Candle works to increase public participation and support in the fight against stillbirth, sudden infant death syndrome (SIDS), and other causes of sudden, unexpected infant death (SUID). The organization provides educational brochures and bereavement materials.

**Josephine DeMello
SIDS Foundation**
PO Box 1712,
Camarillo, CA 93011
(888) 674-2999
fax: (805) 265-5456
e-mail: yolanda@joey
demellofoundation.org
website: www.joey
demellofoundation
.org

The Josephine DeMello SIDS Foundation is a nonprofit organization formed to educate families, friends, and the general public about SIDS, to raise awareness in the community about SIDS, and to support everyone who is touched by SIDS. The organization's website provides information and resources about SIDS. The foundation raises funds through public donations and events such as the annual Joey's Run for Life.

FOR FURTHER READING

Books

John Batt, *Stolen Innocence: A Mother's Fight for Justice: The Story of Sally Clark.* London: Elbury Press, 2004.

Monica Cane, *A Journey to Healing: Life After SIDS.* San Leandro, CA: Jireh, 2004.

Angela Cannings, *Cherished: A Mother's Fight to Prove Her Innocence.* London: Sphere, 2007.

Tara Lang Chapman, *Genetic Heavy Metal Toxicity: Explaining SIDS, Autism, Tourette's, Alzheimer's and Other Epidemics.* New York: iUniverse, 2008.

Sudhansu Chokroverty, *100 Questions About Sleep and Sleep Disorders.* Sudbury, MA: Jones and Bartlett, 2008.

Michael Dean, *Empty Cribs: The Impact of Smoking on Child Health.* Frederick, MD: Arts and Sciences, 2006.

Dawne J. Gurbutt, *Sudden Infant Death Syndrome: Learning from Stories About SIDS, Motherhood and Loss.* Seattle: Radcliffe, 2007.

Richard Hardoin, Judith Henslee, and Carrie Sheehan, *The Voice Within: Premonitions of Sudden Death in Children.* Mustang, OK: Tate, 2007.

Igor Kelmanson, *Sleep and Breathing in Infants and Young Children.* New York: Nova Biomedical Books, 2006.

Karen Martin, *When a Baby Dies of SIDS: The Parents' Grief and Search for Reason.* Walnut Creek, CA: Left Coast Press, 2007.

Paul Offit and Charlotte Moser, *Vaccines and Your Child: Separating Fact from Fiction.* New York: Columbia University Press, 2011.

Giulia Ottaviani, *Crib Death: Sudden Unexplained Death of Infants—the Pathologist's Viewpoint.* Heidelberg, Germany: Springer Verlag, 2007.

R.A. Ruiz, *Coping with the Death of a Brother or Sister.* New York: Rosen, 2001.

Peter Sidebotham and Peter Fleming, *Unexpected Death in Childhood: A Handbook for Practitioners.* Hoboken, NJ: John Wiley & Sons, 2007.

Kathleen Stratton, Donna Almario, Theresa Wizemann, and Marie McCormick, eds., *Immunization Safety Review: Vaccines and Sudden Unexpected Death in Infancy.* Washington, DC: National Academies Press, 2003.

Annie Vickerstaff, *How Safe Is Your Baby? The Facts Behind the Official Advice.* Surrey, UK: White Ladder, 2006.

Periodicals

American Academy of Pediatrics, "The Changing Concept of Sudden Infant Death Syndrome: Diagnostic Coding Shifts, Controversies Regarding the Sleeping Environment, and New Variables to Consider in Reducing Risk," *Pediatrics,* November 2005.

M. Bohnert, M. Grosse Perdekamp, and S. Pollak, "Three Subsequent Infanticides Covered Up as SIDS," *International Journal of Legal Medicine,* January 2005.

Teri Brown, "Can Pacifiers Reduce the Risk of SIDS?," *Babies Today,* Fall 2005.

Joyce Epstein and Clare Jolly, "Credibility Gap? Parents' Beliefs About Reducing the Risk of Cot Death," *Community Practitioner,* November 2009.

Martine Hackett, "Babies Sleep Safest on Their Backs: Race, Resistance and the Consequences of Cultural Competency," paper presented at the annual meeting of the American Sociological Association, Montreal, Canada, August 10, 2006.

Fern Hauck, Olanrewaju Omojokun, and Mir Siadaty, "Do Pacifiers Reduce the Risk of Sudden Infant Death Syndrome?," *Pediatrics,* November 2005.

Ariane Kemkes, "Smothered Infants—Neglect, Infanticide or SIDS? A Fresh Look at the 19th-Century Mortality Schedules," *Human Ecology,* July 11, 2009.

Hannah Kinney and Bradley Thach, "The Sudden Infant Death Syndrome," *New England Journal of Medicine,* August 20, 2009.

Hannah Kinney et al., "The Brainstem and Serotonin in the Sudden Infant Death Syndrome," *Annual Review of Pathology: Mechanisms of Disease*, April 2009.

David Mage and Maria Donner, "A Unifying Theory for SIDS," *International Journal of Pediatrics*, July 23, 2009.

Michael Malloy and Daniel Freeman, "Age at Death, Season, and Day of Death as Indicators of the Effect of the Back to Sleep Program on Sudden Infant Death Syndrome in the United States, 1992–1999," *Archives of Pediatrics & Adolescent Medicine*, April 2004.

Adriene Marshall, "Can Bacterial Infection Explain Some So-Called SIDS Deaths?," *Pulmonary Reviews*, October 2008.

Tom Matthews, "Sudden Unexpected Infant Death: Infanticide or SIDS?," *Lancet*, January 2005.

Rachel Moon, Lauren Kotch, and Laura Aird, "State Child Care Regulations Regarding Infant Sleep Environment Since the Healthy Child Care America—Back to Sleep Campaign," *Pediatrics*, July 14, 2006.

Siri Opdal and Torleiv Rognum, "The Sudden Infant Death Syndrome Gene: Does It Exist?," *Pediatrics*, October 2004.

Fiona Raitt and Suzanne Zeedyk, "Mothers on Trial: Discourses on Cot Death and Munchausen's Syndrome by Proxy," *Feminist Legal Studies*, 2004.

Ruth Rosen, "New Analysis: Regulating Flame Retardant Chemicals," *Berkeley (CA) Daily Planet*, January 28, 2010.

Julie Scelfo, "The Stuffing Dreams Are Made Of?," *New York Times*, January 14, 2009.

Tushar Shah, Kevin Sullivan, and John Carter, "Sudden Infant Death Syndrome and Reported Maternal Smoking During Pregnancy," *American Journal of Public Health*, October 2006.

Carrie Shapiro-Mendoza et al., "US Infant Mortality Trends Attributable to Accidental Suffocation and Strangulation in Bed from 1984 Through 2004: Are Rates Increasing?," *Pediatrics*, February 2009.

BR Sharma, "Sudden Infant Death Syndrome: A Subject of Medicolegal Research," *American Journal of Forensic Medicine & Pathology*, March 2007.

Websites

California SIDS Program (www.californiasids.com).

National Sudden and Unexpected Infant/Child Death and Pregnancy Loss Resource Center (www.sidscenter.org).

Sudden Unexplained Death in Childhood Program (www.sudc.org).

Tiny Handprints (www.tinyhandprints.org).

INDEX